GRACE
LIVING ON THE FRIENDSHIP OF GOD

Stephen Lee

BROADMAN PRESS
Nashville, Tennessee

4254-37
ISBN: 0-8054-5437-3
Dewey Decimal Classification: 253.2
Subject Headings: MINISTERS//CHRISTIAN LIFE//GRACE (THEOLOGY)
Library of Congress Catalog Card Number: 86-32720
Printed in the United States of America

Unless otherwise indicated, Scripture quotations are from the *New American Standard Bible.* Copyright © The Lockman Foundation, 1960, 1962, 1963, 1968, 1971, 1972, 1973, 1975, 1977. Used by permission.

Scripture quotations marked (KJV) are from the King James Version of the Bible.

Library of Congress Cataloging-in-Publication Data

Lee, Stephen, 1949-
  Grace : living on the friendship of God.

  1. Christian life—1960-   . I. Title.
BV4501.2.L4255 1987   248.4   86-32720
ISBN 0-8054-5437-3

*To Sally
by whom God's grace
has been reflected to me*

Preface

You may be asking yourself if this book by a totally unknown development director and erstwhile theological novice will be helpful to you. Perhaps I can help you answer this question by telling you something about the book. It is the story of my collision with the God of Abraham, Isaac, and Jacob, as revealed in Jesus Christ.

I write much of myself because it is the only real way I know of expressing how God has encountered me. My events are not heroic or outstanding. There are times, especially in the places where I write of my vocational struggles, when I am ashamed. But nevertheless, God has arrested me through my life experiences to consider Him. I have, therefore, personalized the book in the hope that Jesus Christ will be more real to you as you see how He has encountered me.

You need to know one other thing about the book: It is full of Scripture verses. I hope this does not bore you or turn you off, but the God of my experience has often encountered me in the words of the Bible.

I accepted God's limitless love because it was revealed for me in the biblical portrayal of Jesus Christ. Later, as I struggled to grow as a Christian, the Scriptures often pointed me to His gracious, undeserved love. The biblical message has always been my primary source of information about God and continues as the canon by which all of my theological thought is informed.

I would like to thank the persons who have stood by me in the midst of my disjointed journey. You know who you are. I love you because you have loved me with the love through which God's grace has been reflected to me. I want to thank my wife, Sally Lee, for standing by me all these years.

Numerous persons have read all or parts of this manuscript. Their suggestions and encouragement have literally changed its nature since I began three or four years ago. Without their help, the labor involved in this effort would have produced a stillborn child. Thanks to all of you. Thanks to Pat Simpson who has faithfully turned my longhand into a representative, typewritten page. Finally, "thanks be to God, who gives us the victory through our Lord Jesus Christ" (1 Cor. 15:57).

Contents

Introduction

Have you ever sat in the limbs of a big oak tree at dusk, and watched the darkness sneak up on the light? It is a strange phenomenon—this falling of evening. All of the shapes and sizes which were so familiar just a few minutes before begin to take on strange and sometimes ominous overtones. The stump a couple of hundred yards away becomes a big buck, and you are not sure what is easing across the field in front of you, despite the fact that a few moments ago it was merely a few head of cattle.

I remember the fear which straightjacketed me as a youth when I walked in from a deer hunt after the night had overwhelmed the day. My widened eyes darted from side to side, and I had to keep telling myself over and over again there was nothing to be afraid of. I finally tried whistling (yes, there is good reason for the phrase, "whistling in the dark") and just hoped those erie shapes that kept popping up out of the ground were the stumps, rocks, and cedar bushes I knew were there and not the bobcats or crazed people of which I was terrified.

My Christian experience has often resembled the shadow behind the reality, and what I thought had substance was only a darkened image of the authentic. I have not seen what was real in the obvious tones of black and white or with great clarity of vision. I have come to believe that life in the semidarkness is the standard for every one of us, whether or not we want to admit it. It was true of the apostle Paul, and he applied it to us: "For we know in part, and we prophesy in part; . . . For now we see in a mirror dimly" (1 Cor. 13:9,12).

The kind of mirror to which we have grown accustomed, which perfectly reflects images, was not developed until the thirteenth century. The kind to which Paul referred was made of metal, polished as brightly as possible. It often rippled with unevenness and became dull with rust and imperfection. The reflections it threw off were only poor facsimiles of the real thing. The true image was reflected through a tarnished and marred medium. What we know of God is like that. He is perfect and pure and loving, but we never get Him undiluted. We only see God's reflection in the dim light of our culture and experiences, none of which portrays Him accurately. His love is lost in the pain of tragedy, and He seems to flee in the face of our disappointments, frustrations, and fears.

But what I have tried to say in this book is that, even though the reflections of God we get in the dim light of our culture and experience are imperfect, we may nevertheless trust in Him. The medium is not perfect; people are dying, the deficit grows larger, and "star wars" insanity rages on. We are lost and lonely in our spirits, often isolated from the persons who could help us the most. There is darkness, pain, confusion, and sin in our world, and yet there is God.

I have watched my daughter die in a recovery room in Houston, suffered with my wife in her protracted illnesses and two surgeries, and wandered in the dimly lit wilderness of vocational indecision and frustration for nine long years. I have begged God to give me a sign to show me what to do—only to be answered with absolute darkness and silence. I have searched and searched and have been left without any real clue as to what occupational socket I should plug in my energies. I have asked Him to please ease the pain of my suffering and hollered at Him that, if He didn't, I was going to throw Him and my feeble little faith into the ground—like a child discarding an empty candy wrapper.

I could not, of course, discard God. He has me, lock, stock, and barrel. I live to please Him; I want to do good, serving my Lord. And that is the point: God was in the dim light of silence and darkness, and the excruciating sorrow of not knowing what to do next. The pain of my daughter's death only gradually receded, and yet He found me in the pain.

I have wanted to die because of the isolation and aloneness I have felt and because I am doing so little good in a world where there is so much bad. The good news of God for me, though, is that He loves me all of the time, in the good and the bad, and even if I don't change the world. I fear I will not, and yet I have found in God's grace the sanity and strength to keep on trying. Read on; maybe you can catch a little glimmer of God's grace and, in so doing, find the strength to be His servant. I would like that very much.

1
Pointing Toward Jesus Only

Every long and arduous excursion needs a compass to point its pilgrims in the direction of their destination. This chapter serves to point you in the direction of simple faith in Jesus alone toward which my journey has taken me.

Starting this trip was easier for me than continuing to my present destination because I wasted a lot of effort along the way. The energy with which I was propelled was the love of God, but the journey was nearly aborted because I was frantically looking for a way to activate the fuel, instead of merely turning on the key!

To change to a rather mundane metaphor: The handle to the grubbing hoe of life is the love of God; unless one uses it, it is impossible to dig a hole with the blade of God's purpose. I nearly missed out because I dissipated my energy trying to get strong enough to dig, instead of simply picking up the handle and swinging the hoe!

God's undeserved love was hard for me to accept because I thought I had to coerce God into caring for me. When my substitutes for simple faith were absorbed in my darkness of sorrow and confusion, I began to understand God loved me as I was. I did not have to pretend with God.

Boil all of the events and experiences of my life down to the pure broth, see, and what you have is one who has found in Christ the only answer to his need for relationship with God. My struggle simmered it down to faith in the living Christ plus none of the supposed certainties of my experience or the cultural expressions of my faith. My feelings paralleled those expressed by a college girl I taught in Sunday School: "I used to be so sure until my father died . . ." Now we have to depend on Christ.

For a time, though, I did not realize the brilliance of God's love was overshadowing me in every circumstance. I kept thinking I had to work for God to turn His light on me. And yet, I found my effort to see His reflection kept blocking the light! It was as if an incandescence flooded the stage of my life, but I did not know it and kept jumping around trying to get in its glow. The only problem was that every time I hopped, I ended up behind a piece of the set, and the brilliance of God's grace was dimmed by my own effort.

I tried to see the light by maintaining a vigorous devotional life. I used to get up very early and try to pray and read my Bible. I thought this would make me worthy to get a glimpse of the reflection—only I did not function well at 5:00 AM and found this was an empty form. Then I tried a devotional time late at night, and after that failed to help me see the light, I started sneaking off to the seminary prayer chapel in the middle of the day to try to read and pray. I could read and pray well then, but I still barely saw a glimmer of God's grace.

I did not understand this because R. A. Torey, whom I had read, assured me if I prayed hard and long enough, and worked hard enough at being worthy, I could see the light! He said I had to: (1) receive Christ: I had done that;

(2) renounce sin: I certainly tried to do that; I went every-where renouncing my sin; (3) openly confess my sin: see above, and, oh yes, I was especially adept at openly con-fessing in revival meetings.

I was also wonderful at getting young people to confess their sins. I remember one convocation, in particular, when I gathered the kids together after everyone else had gone home. I had them at the altar of our semidarkened church building, confessing their's and everyone else's sins. We went on for a long time, and it was quite a frenetic occasion. This caused quite a stir when the music director, who had also attended the meeting and was somewhat buoyed up by it all, took it upon himself the next evening to reprimand all the normal sinners for their sloth and spiritual apathy. They thought he re-vealed some false religious pride by his diatribe, and there was "mrumbling" (a combination of mumbling and rumbling) among the saints!

Torey also said I had to: (4) absolutely surrender to God in all things. I was trying to do this too. Why else would I spend all those hours praying in one spot on my knees? I wanted to have callouses on my knees because I heard great spiritual men of the past did. I had a problem here, though. I always found something else to confess, or to give up, approximately three and one-half minutes after I got up from my prayers. (5) Have an intense desire for the spiritual life: I thought I was plenty covetous for the Spirit. (6) Pray specifically for the infilling of the Spirit: I did this over and over. I even told God I would babble like an idiot if He wanted me to. I thought this showed unusual courage since tongues was seen as incoherent mumbling among most Southern Baptist seminary students. (7) Have faith: Well, all I can say here is that I was sure trying to have faith![1]

Perhaps you've had someone tell you that to see the light you also need to develop a strong devotional life. "Yes, siree, you've been saved by grace through faith. But now that you are, here's what you have to do to grow as a Christian: Read your Bible for an hour every day, and pray in one spot on your knees every morning. You will not grow as a Christian until you do these things in a set pattern."

Brother Lawrence was one who followed similar suggestions made to him by well-meaning friends. He finally grew weary of trying to relate to God like that, threw away all of his additions to Jesus, and decided to just love Him. He wrote of his experience: "After my conversion, many people pressed many various spiritual books and manuals on me, all offering different, and sometimes conflicting advice about the Christian life. Personal devotions, prayers and so on. Faced with all these different ways of going to God, I decided to wash my hands of them all. They only served, it seemed to me to confuse what surely must be an essentially simple thing."[2]

In another letter, Brother Lawrence explained what he decided to do: "I've set myself simply and solely to know and love God himself and to renounce all substitutes and formulas, even religious ones."[3] He could do that because he understood that the magnitude of devotional gymnastics was not what made it possible for him to see the light. Brother Lawrence's faith in the finished work of Christ made it possible for him to "always enjoy an habitual silent and secret conversation of the Spirit with God. It's not as difficult as it sounds, once you get away from the idea that there are set times to pray and set times not to pray."[4]

Brother Lawrence delighted in his fellowship with God ("We are not meant to be cramped, tongue-tied, fearful, and hesitant in the presence of God. The Son has come to set us free."[5]), and he did not denigrate prayer. Neither is it my intention to insinuate prayer is unimportant. I practice prayer; I am struggling to learn to pray without ceasing. I take great delight in my fellowship with Almighty God. I understand with Brother Lawrence, however, that I am not right with God because I pray at any particular time in any particular position.

I learned in my pain that it is my privilege to pray anywhere at anytime without any form and to believe in God's constant presence. My fellowship with God is a response to His light of grace and not a condition for it. This is good news for the laity as well as the paid professional church worker because it means one can experience the love and grace of God even when one is not being paid to sit around and pray.

I also tried to see the light by plunging into a series of religious works. I attended Sunday School and church regularly, I worked on Saturday mornings in a bus outreach program, I tried to talk about Christ to at least one person every day, whether or not they wanted to listen (I didn't always do this, I must confess—I said I tried.), and struggled to give to the church on a regular and consistent basis. The ultimate religious work for me was when I got to pastor my first church. I just knew this would help me see the light, but alas, my vision was not much improved!

I couldn't understand why my vision was not improved since my efforts were in line with the kinds of things

F. B. Meyer said I needed to do to see the light. All I had to do, he said, was:

(1) Possess the Holy Spirit: I was certainly possessed by something, and I assumed it was the Spirit!

(2) Be cleansed: I was trying to be cleansed. I even confessed some sins I didn't commit, so I could be as clean as possible.

(3) Live for the glory of Christ: The kids who rode my bus thought I was Christ!

(4) Make sure my teaching was in harmony with the Word of God: This one bothered me: Was life in the light only for teachers? How did I know whether my teaching conformed to the *true* precepts of the Bible? Why, I had read hundreds of methods of interpretation of the Scriptures just in my time in seminary. How did I know which one of these equally sincere approaches was correct? Was any of them correct? I knew that person after person had disagreed over biblical interpretation, even after using the same, basic hermeneutical principles. Meyer opened up a real can of worms here.

(5) Have faith: Who needed faith with all of the above?

I am not poking fun at what might be important activities. I am simply saying my activities did not help me see the light of God's grace. My fatigue was a friend to me in that it taught me God's grace did not run out when my strength did!

It is very easy for us good folk in the church to assume we'll see the light because we exercise devotional or religious discipline or because we control the money, power, and influence in our communities. This is not true. We aren't fast enough to catch the reflection of God's grace in our own strength!

The church which fails to remember this proclaims the

good news, which is for sinners, to people who cannot hear it because they are working too hard at trying to be good enough to deserve it. This limits the gospel to "good people" and encourages legalists to so concentrate on their little toy list of externals that they cannot hear God calling them to love persons who do not meet this criteria. Their works, which are purportedly done to serve God, create the ultimate in pride and selfishness. To these kinds of people Jesus said: "You are like whitewashed tombs which on the outside appear beautiful, but inside they are full of dead men's bones and all uncleanness. Even so you too outwardly appear righteous to men, but inwardly you are full of hypocrisy and lawlessness" (Matt. 23:27-28).

Ben Bledsoe tried a combination of devotional and religious works and faith in Christ to put himself right with God. The tasks by which he hoped to gain God's favor were: "Read and study my Bible daily, pray on my knees every morning, attend every church meeting scheduled, try to win at least one person per day for Christ, and tithe."[6] I identify with his effort. I have been immersed in all of these activities, hoping I was forcing God to use me. I knew deep down, however, there was no point of achievement at which I earned God's blessing. I could never pray enough, read my Bible enough, or go to church enough to see the light! "The legalist shares the futility of Sisyphus, the crafty and avaricious being of Corinth, who was condemned in Hades to push a large stone up a hill, only to have it roll back again."[7]

Bledsoe finally discovered that he could not work his way to God, after a struggle in which he was divided between allegiance to Christ and allegiance to himself. He fell back on two assurances: "One, God loves me in

Christ without me doing anything to deserve it. Two, God
lives in me because I've received Him, not because I'm
good."[8]

Some persons who try to be worthy of the reflection of
God's grace don't fare as well as Bledsoe. A man in the
Hamilton church I pastored was driven away from the
church by the burdens he had added to faith. He simply
burned out after simultaneously holding three or four
major jobs in the church for an extended period of time.
This sad experience vitally affected the man's two sons
who were never baptized into our fellowship after their
expression of faith because their father showed no interest in having them repeat his kind of bondage.

This, to me, points to one of the primary reasons people
leave the church. It is not because they were not involved
in the church's activities (This viewpoint results in the
curious practice in some churches of appointing un-
qualified persons to teach Sunday School in an effort to
get them to attend). *It is because the church changes its
message from grace to works.*

For instance, a man I taught in a seminar told me some
friends in a prayer group he once attended told him that
he didn't have to quit smoking to become a Christian. God
loved him just the way he was, they said. He then accepted God's unconditional acceptance, only to be told he
needed to quit smoking! The man's friends explained this
by saying that God was not pleased when Christians
smoked. They even organized their prayer time around
supplication for him to drop that nasty habit.

Questions began to pound in the man's brain: *Did God
love me as a smoking non-Christian but not as a smoking
Christian? Does God's unconditional acceptance stop at
the point of conversion?* He withdrew for awhile from the

overt pressures of his friends to try to figure all this out. He eventually decided that they were wrong and that God loved him whether or not he smoked. He did not smoke when I met him. He had decided to quit when he was ready—seemed he was not totally interested in developing lung cancer!

My experience with trying to work my way into God's favor led me to the Scriptures as I began to tire and to realize I could not be worthy of God. I discovered I could receive God's love by faith alone. "For I am not ashamed of the gospel, for it is the power of God for salvation to everyone who believes, . . . For in it the righteousness of God is revealed from faith to faith" (Rom. 1:16-17). I was impressed the continuous reflection of God's grace was not obtained by "progressing" from faith to faith plus works. I was glad to know that just as I received the light by faith, I could continue to enjoy its glow by simple acceptance of its brilliance. "As it is written, 'But the righteous man shall live by faith' " (Rom. 1:17).

The Bible affirmed for me that my works were not the reason I was experiencing God's grace. "Where then is boasting? It is excluded. By what kind of law? Of works? No, but by a law of faith. For we maintain that a man is justified by faith apart from works of the Law" (Rom. 3:27-28). My pride was shot in the death of my own illusion of worthiness, and I came to see only God could bring me into relationship with Him "that He [God] might be just and the justifier of the one who has faith in Jesus" (Rom. 3:26).

I found, then, in the bankruptcy of my own efforts, how much I needed Jesus. "The Law has become our tutor to lead us to Christ, that we may be justified by faith" (Gal. 3:24). My own personal law, embodied in some biblical

teachings, cultural and church mores, and demands I
made on myself, drove me to see the light by realizing
there was no way I could meet its criteria. My legalism,
and then my certitude about God's direction in my life,
gave way to the realities of my journey.

I found out I am not God and cannot take God's own
ultimate place in my life. He has called me to come to the
end of myself so that I can trust in His holy love alone.
Jesus Christ plus nothing is the establisher of the New
Covenant of faith. There is nothing beyond Him, or above
Him, with which I must humor Him to love me. He already loves me since He is the Revealer of the Father's
love to which nothing can or must be added.

I found my experience of Jesus-plus-nothing was a parable of the experience of the early disciples. There was a
great struggle in the church to decide whether faith in
Christ alone was the essence of what they believed. Their
leaders gathered in Jerusalem to come to a consensus of
opinion about this, and some of those present wanted to
tell the Gentiles their faith in Christ was not enough to
save them.[9] Those persons felt the new converts needed
to be circumcised and obey the Law to be in good standing
in the church. Peter said to them:

> Brethren, you know that in the early days God made a choice
> among you, that by my mouth the Gentiles should hear the word
> of the gospel and believe. And God, who knows the heart, bore
> witness to them, giving them the Holy Spirit, just as He also did
> to us; and He made no distinction between us and them, cleans-
> ing their hearts by faith. Now therefore why do you put God to
> the test by placing upon the neck of the disciples a yoke which
> neither our fathers nor we have been able to bear? But we
> believe that we are saved through the grace of the Lord Jesus,
> in the same way as they also are (Acts 15:7-11).

That statement of faith is one of the high-water marks of the church, and is surely one of the best pieces of news I have ever seen! I did not have to merit God's love! He had cleansed me of my sin! He had set me free to trust in Him alone for the love of God! "The heart cleansing which is so assiduously cultivated, God grants; the Holy Spirit Who is so scrupulously sought, God gives—and the *means is simply the divine gospel which is the power of God unto salvation*"[10] (author's italics).

I was not a creator of the light. I was only a receiver and reflector of it. I didn't have to carry the burden of trying to be worthy of God. I was not doomed to await the light until I accomplished a long list of tasks or got it all together. I rather had the thrill of accepting God's reflection of grace in Christ in the now to illumine my pathway for the future.

I am not saying I have abandoned all concern for my actions. I am saying I did not see the light of God's grace because of what I did or did not do. No amount of striving to be worthy of His light put me into relationship with Him. "When they [the Reformers] preached justification by grace alone through faith alone, they were driving home the point that actions motivated by law could not bring about the interpersonal relationship which God sought with His children."[11]

This relationship with God through simple faith in Christ has bound me to Him in loving fellowship. I used to fear that the acceptance of God's grace would set me free to wreak havoc on the world because of my freedom. However, I have decided if I am ever going to be a decent human being it is because God's love has caused me to try to follow Him. We can trust God's love to capture us.

This was enforced for me by a story I heard about an

old-time preacher who always rode shotgun on the stagecoach on which he traveled because he liked to see the
country and visit with the driver. On one particular
route, he noticed that when the horses came to a specific
point in the road they panicked in terror. They would rise
up and claw the air, oblivious to the fact the stagecoach
was going all over the trail. This scared the passengers
and jeopardized the route's success.

One day when the preacher rode that route everything
was different, however. The driver later explained that
the horses no longer spooked because he popped them on
the nose with a whip when they came to the spot in the
road where they had previously been frightened. They
were concentrating on their stinging noses rather than
on their fear! This is an analogy of what happened to me
when I saw the light. I got something else on my mind
besides sin, condemnation, hate, worry, and confusion.
God discovered me, gained my love through His amazing,
unmerited favor, and propelled me into the world to be a
reflector of His grace. I serve Him in faith and love, because "the love of Christ controls [me]" (2 Cor. 5:14).

My works are not born in an effort to try to make
myself worthy of God's light in Christ. They are a reflection of Him who shows God's grace so brilliantly that He
died a thief's death so that I might enjoy His fellowship.
It is the motivating reflection of God's love in Christ to
which Paul referred when he wrote that God works in us,
"both to will and to work for His good pleasure" (Phil.
2:13).

I have decided, therefore, that the motivation to live as
I do is the key to whether my works are the gold of Christian service or the hay and stubble of legalistic compulsion. My behavior may be the endless effort of legalism,

or it may be the outflow of grace. Luther confirmed this when he said that one who performed works because he was trying to be good enough to see the light of God's grace was living under the law, but one who served out of the overflow of the light one had already seen was living under grace.

I also tried to maintain a high level of emotional euphoria to be worthy to see the light of God's grace in Christ. I heard and read after many people who said a real Christian was always happy. Their attitude was: "Good Christians do not live by faith alone; they must have ecstasy!"

I was able to maintain this kind of facade until Karin died—then all of my hypocritical joy came tumbling in around me. I had a hard time reconciling my grief and despair with the idea that I was suppoed to be happy all the time. How was I to be happy: the light of my life had gone out! My feelings were reflected in the Psalm: "Answer me quickly, O Lord, my spirit fails;/Do not hide Thy face from me,/Lest I become like those who go down to the pit./Deliver me, O Lord, . . ./I take refuge in Thee" (Ps. 143:7,9). But there was no deliverance—only tears and grief.

Was I to believe the light of God's grace was snuffed out for me because the joy I thought I ought to feel was ripped from me by the chilled hands of separation, loneliness, and defeat, having fought so hard only to be beaten by the relentless sorrow of death? Was I alienated from God? Had He separated Himself from me? No! No! A thousand times no! I came to recognize God loved me no matter how I felt.

Paul never told his converts they had to be giddy all the time. On his first evangelistic tour, "After they had

preached the gospel to that city [Derbe] and had made
many disciples, they returned to Lystra and to Iconium
and to Antioch, strengthening the souls of the disciples,
encouraging them to *continue in the faith*" (Acts 14:21-22,
author's italics). Then he told them, "Through many
tribulations we must enter the kingdom of God" (v. 22).

Bruner, in commenting on this passage, wrote, "Between baptism and the coming of the Kingdom there is no
necessary second experience (received after performing
'enough' works). But there are many difficulties."[12] He
was saying, with Paul, that there is never a point in our
lives when godliness immunizes us from hardship. The
assurance that all of our problems will be solved when we
accept Jesus as Savior is false. We can accept Paul's
warning that troubles will come. They are not a sign that
God has withdrawn Himself from us; they are a part of
the territory that comes with living in an imperfect
world. God doesn't take us out of common human experience; He does enable us to live through these experiences
by faith in the Light.

I think the crux of the matter is that some of us aren't
satisfied with Jesus and feel we need some elevated, ec-
static experience to help us tolerate our faith. At least
this is the feeling I got from some of what I used to read.
It was as if simple faith in Jesus Christ, the Lord of life,
was not sufficient for God's grace. People kept telling me
I needed a second experience, or another experience, outside of the one I had with Christ. Why? Isn't fellowship
with Almighty God through Christ His Son enough? It is
for me.

Those who believe the light of God's grace is reflected
only in euphoria are in for a shock or are hopelessly
hypocritical because happiness comes and goes. The state

of my emotions are more often a reflection of how things are going with me, rather than a gauge of whether I am in the brilliance of God's love.

Elation was a morning mist in the rising desert sun in my moments of grief and loss. Only the reality of what God had done for me in Christ was steadfast. He will stand forever, even after the ashes of charred dreams have long since been lost to the wind. God is real; He has put us right with Himself. I, for one, would rather know I am right with Him by the reflection of grace in the cross and resurrection than by the measure of ecstasy I am able to maintain.

Actually, life is a conglomeration of hilarity and sorrow and all gradations in between. Our experience with our children is a verification of this for me. Our grief was compounded after Karin's death when the doctors told us we couldn't have any more children. You can imagine our joy when Sally discovered she was pregnant again and when our son was born!

We decided to include *Isaac* as a part of the baby's name, since the biblical Isaac was not supposed to be born either (his parents were too old) and since the English translation of the word means "laughter." His birth was certainly a happy moment for us after the grinding pressure of the preceding two years. We accepted him as a gift from God and now know him as Ike. He is sensitive, intelligent, strong willed (like his mama), a fine basketball player, and a blossoming pianist.

Later, another great and new joy entered our lives when Andrea Joyce Lee became a part of our family at seven weeks of age. I had mentioned that Sally and I would like to have another child to a friend in our church, who worked for a local children's agency. We filled out all

the paperwork and waited. Her sister, who also worked
for the agency, called me one evening after work and said
she had a baby girl for us!

I still recall the pounding of my heart and the rush of
my emotions as I realized what she was saying. We were
elated when this beautiful baby girl entered our home,
and we are amused and overjoyed by her happy and elfish
membership in our family.

She is a Lee through and through and is lively, energet-
ic, and resilient in an overcoming way. She simply will
not let her daddy's fussing get her down! I could not
possibly love her more. Sally and I are grateful to have
"Laughter" and Andrea around the house, and I am
grateful for the health my family has experienced since
the cacophony of bad news of 1974-1976.

So I have decided life is a kaleidoscope of good and bad,
joy and pain, righteousness and evil. This is the nature of
the beast upon which I have been set. I am struggling to
come to terms with this and to ask for strength and love
to give it my best shot, instead of asking to be removed
from the fracas!

Devotional disciplines, religious works, and emotional
ecstasy were all means I used to try to buy God's favor.
I am sure you could add some creative efforts to my list.
You might as well stop because the only way to enjoy
God's grace is through simple faith in Jesus alone.

The issue is, you see, in what will we trust, our own
strength or the brilliant reflection of God's grace in Jesus
Christ? We cannot live divided against ourselves, mouth-
ing that we see the light of grace but trusting in our
works. Luther said with mutual dependence on Christ
and in the law, "Faith and the whole Christ crash to the
ground . . . For the two—Christ and supplements—do not

suffer each other together in the heart so that I rest my trust on both; one must get out of there: either Christ or my own doing."[13]

I have decided to trust in Christ, plus nothing. All else is ashes. He is the greatest reflection of God's grace I have ever seen, so I will cling simply and solely to Him alone. "My faith has found a resting place,/Not in device nor creed;/ . . . ./It is enough that Jesus died,/And that he died for me."[14]

Notes

1. Frederick Dale Bruner, *A Theology of the Holy Spirit* (Grand Rapids: William B. Eerdmans, 1970), pp. 323-344 analyzes authors related to this subject.

2. Brother Lawrence, paraphrased in David Winter, "Closer Than a Brother," *Bookshorts*, Aug./Sept. 1977, pp. 60-63. This is a collection of Brother Lawrence's personal correspondence.

3. Ibid.

4. Ibid.

5. Ibid.

6. Ben Bledsoe, "Finally, Freedom for Me," *The Baptist Program*, Sept. 1976, p. 6.

7. Richard A. Batey, *Thank God I'm OK* (Nashville: Abingdon, 1976), p. 55.

8. Bledsoe, p. 6.

9. Bruner, pp. 198-204,214-215, gives an excellent discussion of the Jerusalem Council and the apostolic messages in Acts. I am indebted to him for his thought-provoking work on the struggle of the New Testament church to decide what they considered essential for salvation.

10. Ibid., p. 201.

11. William Hordern, *Living By Grace* (Philadelphia: The Westminster Press, 1975), pp. 38.

12. Bruner, p. 199.

13. Ibid., p. 204.

14. Lidie H. Edmunds, "My Faith Has Found a Resting Place," *Baptist Hymnal* (Nashville: Convention Press, 1975), no. 380.

2
The Start
of an Awesome Journey

There was a man at Wimbledon

> "Who went to the tennis matches
> And propped a TV set on his knees,
> So he could watch the action
> Without having to turn his head
> Right left right left,"[1]

and there was another man

> "At quite another court
> Who watched from a safe distance
> The trial by Pilate
> And the actions that led to
> Golgotha."[2]

My own life with Christ has been anything but a spectator sport. I have been totally immersed and overwhelmed by our daily contention since I first committed to accept His offer of fellowship, as a freshman at Sam Houston State University. Ours has been anything but a placid and passive relationship.

Sally and I first began to understand the Christian life might entail some pain and struggle after we moved to the rural community of Hamilton, Texas, where I assumed the pastorate of Calvary Baptist Church. I was called to this place of service while a student at Southwestern Baptist Theological Seminary in Fort Worth, Texas. Sally was five months pregnant, and on April 16, 1974, in a small hospital in Clifton, Texas, she gave birth to our first child. We named her Karin Elizabeth Lee and were overjoyed by her entry into our lives. Our joy and excitement was subdued, however, when we discovered she had a congenital heart defect.

We first knew something was wrong when the nurses would not let us see Karin after her birth. This was unusual since Sally was supposed to be breast feeding. Two days later, the nurses, encouraged by cries of "I want to see my baby," finally brought her to Sally. We noticed she was a little blue around the mouth, and the authorities told us they had arranged a visit for us with a Waco cardiologist. Our worst fears were realized when he told us Karin had a hole in the upper chamber of her heart. He called it a ventricle septical defect.

Karin's strength increased for the first eight months of her life, during which time we took her to Houston for a heart catheterization. This time was a roller coaster of hope and fear: We hoped she would continue to grow and get stronger for surgery; we feared she would die at any moment. I tiptoed into her room many times during the night to see if she were still breathing. We continued to care for her and our church. I drove 180 miles round trip to the seminary three to four days a week until this routine was interrupted by Sally's chronic fatigue. There was something beyond being tired involved here, even though she was certainly weary from constantly caring for Karin.

So Sally went to see a physician who, after the several

tests, told us she had a tumor on her thyroid gland. My poor wife—she already had a critically ill daughter—now she had a tumorous thyroid! The doctor assured us it was probably benign, but he could not be sure until surgery. So in October 1974, she had a thyroidectomy which confirmed that the tumor was benign.

We were grateful Sally did not have cancer but were still feeling numb and emotionally drained. We had been living under the illusion that life with Christ was always a mountaintop experience, and April through October 1974 had definitely had its share of valleys! The pain was an intrusion into our castle of certitude.

This shook me up because the clear boundary lines for my Christian experience were quickly becoming distorted. But it slowly began to dawn on me that Sally and I did not have to wait until we worked everything out to enjoy God's fellowship. Jesus' last words from the cross—"It is finished"—were His benediction on His work for the salvation of humanity, and this assured us Jesus had set us apart for Himself despite the fact we were quickly loosing the ability to hold onto Him. He had sought us and entered into relationship with us as individuals, despite our growing personal consternation. Out of the darkness of the demolition of our supposed surefire Christian experiences, we turned to the bright light of Christ.

The assurance of my fellowship with Christ despite the dimness of my family's illness became very important to me. I realized the various things which I thought would always solidify my relationship with Jesus were idols doomed to fail in the face of the gloom of the darkness of physical infirmity. The essence behind their form was Jesus Christ alone.

This corresponded for me to the fulfillment of Old Testament purification by an inner relationship with God which I had come to know in Jesus Christ. The failure of my certitude, based upon particular externals, corresponded to the failure of shadows and form presented in the Scriptures.

> The New Testament repudiated the whole body of purity laws. You see ideas of cleanness change a great deal under the Christ and His contemporaries. Jesus made a clear distinction between ritual goodness and moral goodness. Ritual goodness or cleanness was based on outside elements. Moral goodness arose from an inner relationship with God.[3]

Jesus' ultimate and final sacrifice for sin made this inner relationship an immediate reality for me despite the failure of certain practices or beliefs I had always clung to as necessary for Christian faith. "By this will [Jesus' death on the cross] we have been sanctified through the offering of the body of Jesus Christ once for all. For by one offering He has perfected for all time those who are sanctified" (Heb. 10:10,14).

I began to see the light of Christ behind the dullness of the medium through which I had always thought He would be transmitted. In actuality, some of these beliefs, practices, or cultural transmissions of the eternal Christ made up a personal prison in which He had been trapped by my limited experience of Him. The uncertainty I began to feel about the specifics of my faith freed Him from the penitentiary of my expectations and helped me to begin to trust Him alone.

I was encouraged in my dependence on Jesus alone by Paul's reference to the recipients of his correspondence as saints, despite their moral lapses and spiritual immaturity. For instance, he referred to the Corinthians as "holy ones" despite the fact they were morally deficient. There were cavernous divisions within their fellowship; many were abusing their spiritual gifts; confusion was rampant about how they were to relate their faith to worldly practices; and one person was having an affair with his father's wife (stepmother)!

Paul still wrote to these people as persons set apart to a morally righteous and gracious God: "And such were some of you; but you were washed, but you were sanctified, but you were justified in the name of the Lord Jesus Christ, and in the Spirit of our God" (1 Cor. 6:11). "But by his doing you are in Christ Jesus, who became [past tense] to us wisdom from God, and righteousness and sanctification, and redemption" (1 Cor. 1:30). I figured if they were God's in the midst of their problems, then surely I was also His!

This is true for you, too, as one of God's children. Your sanctification is once for all from God's side and is finished and complete in God's eyes. I know this seems incredible to those of you who are awash in your sins and imperfections and who are ravaged by indecision and frustration. I found it bizarre to think God saw me as a finished example of His grace in the midst of the confusion, grief, and doubt of our family's suffering, and yet I began to believe it was true. God began to show me through the exhaustion of my own efforts that being set apart for Him was not something I earned but was rather a gift of His grace, just like every other aspect of the Christian life. We do not deserve to be holy from God's perspective, and yet He gives us His holiness! Christ's death and resurrection is the reflection of God's grace that assures us so.

I had come to believe very early in my experience that

growth was essential for the Christian. The Bible was plain about that: "He who began a good work in you will perfect it until the day of Christ Jesus" (Phil. 1:6). "But we all, with unveiled face beholding as in a mirror the glory of the Lord, are being transformed into the same image [God's] from glory to glory, just as from the Lord, the Spirit" (2 Cor. 3:18). My other reading also confirmed this: "The Christian, the saint-who-is-also-continually-re-pentant-sinner, is on pilgrimage. Aided by what He (God) has revealed, Christians are to move through their lives toward the goal."[4]

This growth was fine with me, as long as it meant only a deepening of my same old commitments and ideas. But radical differences were ahead as what I thought was ultimate and final reality gave way to the events of these days. It seemed everything which was not tied down began to fly all over the place, like the time my brother, Dad, and I were trying to get back home in a windstorm in the middle of Baffin Bay! We bounced so hard the speckled trout we had caught were coming out of the trash can in which we had them stored and Dad's glasses flew off his head. He couldn't stand up but could not sit down, and water was pouring in over the top of the boat. I have since laughed many times about that experience, but it was not funny when it happened.

This storm is an illustration corresponding to Sally and my experience. The only constants in our journey were our commitments to each other and to our Lord, and even the nature of these commitments changed!

"Christian growth" was not simply digging deeper the same old hole on which I had been working but having the ends kicked out of my rut so that I began to change deep down in my spirit, attitude, and commitments. It

meant that I actually began to be open to God's Spirit, to
depend on Him and not on the legalisms and accoutre-
ments to Christian faith on which I had depended for my
Christian growth.

I began to see that sanctification was not trust in reading the Bible or praying but in truly being changed by
Him who is the subject of the Bible and to whom I prayed.
It did me no good to sanctimoniously pray and read Scripture if I refused to let God cleanse me of the greed and
pride which drove me to strive for the biggest and most
visible church or position in my denomination! I began to
feel more of a commitment to the Person of my faith and
not to the things of my faith.

But I could not change my attitude and spirit by myself.
This, too, I discovered was a work of God's grace. "Trans-
formation is a work of grace just as much as the initial
experience when we become children of God."[5] I did not
deserve to grow—it was the gift of life in Christ and was
accomplished by His power. I began to realize this in my
journey, as my struggle drove me deeper into the pages
of the Bible. The passages which were especially mean-
ingful to me were:

1. *"For it is God who is at work in you,* both to will and
to work for His good pleasure" (Phil. 2:13, author's italics).

2. "Peter, an apostle of Jesus Christ, to those who reside
as aliens, . . . chosen according to the foreknowledge of
God the Father, *by the sanctifying work of the Spirit,* that
you may obey Jesus Christ" (1 Pet. 1:1-2, author's italics).

3. "How much more will the blood of Christ, who
through the eternal Spirit offered Himself without blem-
ish to God, *cleanse your conscience from dead works to
serve the living God?"* (Heb. 9:14, author's italics).

I found that the cleansing of my conscience made it possible for me to trust God's ongoing work in my life by continuing to trust in His grace despite how badly I sometimes felt. I guarantee you I did not feel too holy while I sat in the doctor's office and watched my wife weep from the pain of an extremely difficult delivery and the news that our baby girl could die at any moment. And yet the Bible said we were set apart to God and that He was active in our lives.

God, Himself the security, was the Light which shown in the darkness of the insecurity of these times. He gave me the hope to continue the journey despite the fear which had affixed itself to me like the slime on the bottom of a boat hull. This kind of trust in the finished work of Christ as the trigger for personal growth was expressed by Dale Bruner when he wrote: "Sanctification is simply taking justification seriously."[6]

I have not found it simple to take God's constant and continuous care seriously! The doubts, fears, anxiety, and fatigue we experienced in the first months after Karin's birth made everything complicated and hard. Yet behind all of the pain there was God, and He kept pulling me along. Indeed, He was working in the distress to keep me going. "When we are helpless, there he is. He doesn't start your stalled car for you; he comes and sits with you in the snowbank."[7] The brightest light in the shadows of medicine, doctors, hospitals, sleeplessness, worry, and wide-eyed terror was my fellowship with Christ.

The start of my journey was, therefore, begun in the shambles of my trust in my abilities, beliefs, and experiences. I found behind my disillusionment the reality of the living and eternal Christ, who has continued to walk with me down what often appears to be an endless and fright-filled road.

Sally and I began our journey without any real understanding of what kind of trip it would be. I wish I could say the shadows of my own experience and attitudes were always the perfect reflection of the holiness with which God saw me. I'm afraid it was not so. I have been set apart, but I am still in process. I am on the way, but He is not finished with me yet. The reflection you see in me is only a dim imitation of the real thing. And yet, I do see some light on the pilgrimage. It is found in Jesus Christ.

Notes

1. Quentin Payne, "The Spectator," unpublished poem, 2 July 1984. Used by permission of the author.

2. Ibid.

3. Harold Warlick, *Liberation from Guilt* (Nashville: Broadman Press, 1976), p. 68.

4. Seward Hiltner, "Salvation in Dynamic Perspective," *Southwestern Journal of Theology,* 20, No. 2 (Spring 1978), p. 55.

5. T. B. Maston, *Real Life in Christ* (Nashville: Broadman Press, 1974), p. 30.

6. Fredrick Dale Bruner, *A Theology of the Holy Spirit* (Grand Rapids: William B. Eerdman's, 1970), p. 234.

7. Robert Farrar Capon, *The Third Peacock* (Garden City, Doubleday, 1971), pp. 91-92.

3
Living on the Friendship of God

The crisis of our lives began on the evening of our fourth anniversary, January 16, 1975, when Karin entered into congestive heart failure. She began to have great difficulty breathing while lying down because her lungs would fill with fluid. During the night, Sally and I rotated times of holding her in an upright position to try to help her breathe better and to alleviate some of the pressure on her laboring heart. Trips to Waco to the hospital became more frequent with the length of stays getting longer and longer. She needed increased oxygen and medication.

These days and nights were excruciating and exhausting. I was trying to finish my last semester of Master of Divinity work in Fort Worth in addition to pastoring my church, being a husband to my wife, and a father to our sick little girl. My life was filled with sleepless or restless nights at home or hospital, studying on the road as I drove, and stumbling in evenings in Hamilton only to find we had to readmit Karin to the hospital in Waco. Sally was trying to do her best to hold us all together.

Karin's condition deteriorated so quickly we made the decision for her to have surgery much sooner than we had anticipated. We wanted to wait until she had grown and

weighed forty-five pounds or so; but with her worsening
illness, we feared she would not live that long.

We admitted her for surgery at Saint Luke's Children's
Hospital in Houston on March 27 when she was eleven
months old. The procedure to repair the VSD was a complete success, but an inflammation in the inner lining of
her heart (the reason for heart failure) had left it so weak-
ened it could not resume beating after the operation. She
died on March 29, the day after surgery. We laid her tiny
body in the ground on the cold, wet, and misty Saturday
before Easter 1975, in a Hamilton cemetery.

I wore a white suit in the funeral service to symbolize
our victory over death and preached the next day on "The
Hope of Easter." Everyone was proud of how well I held
up. It was due to ignorance and not to strength. I had no
idea how badly Sally and I would hurt in the days ahead.

In May, after Karin's death in March, a doctor told
Sally she had endometriosis, which might make it impossible for her to have another baby. You can imagine our
chagrin and amazement. We had just buried our only
child; how could it be that we could not create another
baby? Was this some kind of cruel joke? Surely we were
only dreaming and would awaken soon!

I was beginning to feel like a person walking the streets
of Mardi Gras where each image one sees is more gro-
tesque and horrible than the previous one. We fooled
them all and ourselves, though, when Windle Isaac Lee
was born to us one day after my birthday on March 18,
1976. What a joy he is!

In the middle of all this, a call came from City View
Baptist Church in Wichita Falls, Texas, to become their
pastor. We decided to go and assumed that pastorate on
November 6, 1976. Sally's health again became a cause of

concern after our move (Here we go again!). She was having a lot of pain, and after an examination, her physician told us her endometriosis had become extremely severe. He said surgery was the only answer to her growing physical discomfort. On his advice and in a desire to rid herself of constant pain, she had a total hysterectomy at the age of twenty-five.

We assumed we could not have any more children in our family, and my eyes began to glaze over like a fighter who is out on his feet. He is trained to stand, no matter how much punishment he has taken. He then begins to take tremendous shots to the head and is helpless to do anything about it. He often stumbles backward on rubberized legs after a hit, instead of going down. His head flys backward, his hands fall to his side, and he rebounds with a disgusting forward tilt, his face exposed to the next smash it will surely receive.

I was an emotional punch-drunk fighter in those days who had no time to withdraw to try to recover from the battle. Heart failure: wham! Unending travel: boom! Exhaustion: whack! Surgery: oof! Death: crash! bang! boom! Endometriosis: bam! Childless: baboom! New baby but no more: finali!

On and on it went, and I knew I had to find some rest and comfort, even though I had to continue driving to school, studying, pastoring, and trying to be a husband and father. I was in reality more like a slush ball than a fighter.

I found time to cry—the trips back and forth to school were excellent for this—and I began to believe Jesus was really my Friend. My conversations with Him kept me sane in this time of shadows and surrealism, as He was always there to hear my cries of pain. I begged Him for help, and I cried out to Him for strength in the only way I had to vent the cauldron of emotions that erupted from the depths of my despair.

I was encouraged to let it all out in this dynamic engagement with my Friend by what I had read in the Bible about His nature and character. I believed God welcomed me with open arms no matter in what emotional or spiritual state I found myself, so I did not withhold anything from Him. I believed that Jesus loved me no matter what and that He was my truest friend. "No longer do I call you slaves; for the slave does not know what his master is doing; but I have called you friends" (John 15:15).

Jesus showed me the brilliant reflection of God's love in the cross and revealed the unbridled wrecklessness with which He would pursue my friendship. Jesus' death showed me I was forgiven of my sins and set apart for relationship with Him and was the ultimate reflection of His desire to eliminate the barrier of sin which had separated me from Him. I was reconciled to Him because I was forgiven. He and I were and are friends because He destroyed the fear which for so long had caused me to withhold myself from Him.

The messages of Paul to Gentile readers became more personal to me as I realized God loved me and this was the evidence I needed to give myself to Him. "God was in Christ reconciling the world to Himself, not counting their trespasses against them" (2 Cor. 5:19). "He has now reconciled you [that meant me!] in his fleshly body through death, in order to present you before Him holy and blameless and beyond reproach" (Col. 1:22). I was able to come to God as a friend because "the good news of the gospel is that God takes the sinfulness of men into Himself, and overcomes in His own heart what cannot be overcome in human life."[1] The separation and alienation from God I felt had been overcome by the revelation of God's love in the cross. I saw that God did not command me as a vicious overlord, rather He walked with me in my journey as a Friend.

God did this solely because He wanted to. God's character was revealed in the cross. "God was in Christ reconciling the world to Himself" (2 Cor. 5:19). Gustaf Aulen put it this way: "Reconciliation between the two hostile parties is based entirely on the activity of one party—the God of love."[2] God was not separate and apart from Jesus, hatefully demanding satisfaction for my sin. He was in Christ, lovingly giving of Himself that I might be in His fellowship.

This was great and marvelous and wonderful good news for me. It pulled me into the everlasting and ever-loving arms of God during the tragedy of Karin's death. I knew I could take advantage of our friendship because He told me so. I often wailed out at Him during this time, only to find after I had quietened that He was still present as my Friend. He did not leave me or take exception to my hatred, fear, and anxiety. He only loved me in the midst of the turmoil, and He welcomed me as a companion. Only God can do that.

I guess what I am trying to say in all of this is, "I ain't afraid of God no more!" He is a gracious and kind and loving God. He is the good God, who has not caused the bad times of my life but rather has sustained and comforted me in their midst. I could not have given myself in friendship to Him if I feared He would pelt me with pain and misfortune in anger over my failures and disobedience. God has come in Christ to assure me that He is the

Friend who will not coerce me into following Him, rather He will love me into His fellowship.

For me, this means the "wrath of God" has nothing to do with divine retributive anger.[3] Romans 5:9 reads: "Much more then, having now been justified by His blood, we shall be saved from the wrath of God." But the words *of God* are not in the original Greek text of the New Testament. They were put in by translators to make the English read more smoothly. The verse, when translated without deference to English, reads: "Much more then, having now been justified by His blood, we shall be saved from the wrath through Him." "The wrath," therefore, is not a part of the emotional makeup of God; it is a technical term that describes God's impersonal power of righteousness at work in the universe. It is His holiness, woven into the fabric of the cosmos.

You might well ask, "Well then, if bad things don't happen to me because God is angry with me, why do they happen?" This is a good question: I have asked many such questions myself as I have wrestled with Him in my problems and distress. There is nothing wrong with asking hard questions of God; how else can we learn anything?

But I have decided I cannot know everything in the dim light of my culture and experience. I am not God: I am just a human, who sees only shadows and images of God's grace in this world. I am not sure, therefore, that there is a good answer to the question of why bad things happen. I know there are not one or two simple solutions to this dilemma which will meet all of your needs. This is especially true if you demand absolute certainty to all the world's problems. Solomon was going to solve the puzzle of the ways things were and ended up crying out: "Vanity of vanities! All is vanity" (Eccl. 1:2).

I do know it was a great weight off of the shoulders of my psyche to know "the wrath of God" was not a reference to one of God's personal emotions, the control of which He occasionally lost at my great personal distress! Bad things happen to me, not because God is angry with me but because I live in a world where these kinds of things happen. Jesus and the disciples encountered a man born blind. The disciples assumed either he or the man's family had committed a sin which so angered God that He punished the man with blindness. They asked Jesus, "Rabbi, who sinned, this man or his parents, that he should be born blind?" (John 9:2). Jesus said that the blindness was not a result of anyone's sin, "but it was in order that the works of God might be displayed in him" (John 9:3). I was delighted to know God was not out to get me when I did bad. This gave me hope to continue believing in the love of God even when Sally was sick or Karin was dying.

I have heard some TV preachers say that illness and sickness are caused by God. I simply don't believe this; I don't believe Jesus believed it! God did not cause Karin's illness and death or Sally's struggle with ill health. I don't see how any honest human being, observing the calamity and suffering of godly people, could say that God caused their pain. I understand to say this would be very profitable, especially if one convinced these sufferers one had the power to overcome their illnesses—if only they would contribute to one's "ministry." The one who makes this promise always has a way to exonerate oneself in case the sufferer is not healed. He or she can simply say the sufferer did not have enough faith and protect oneself from liability over this phoney baloney.

I was a pastor in Wichita Falls when the largest recorded tornado in history swept through our city on April 10, 1977. The town looked as if it had been bombed. Twenty thousand persons were instantly homeless. Forty-six persons were killed. Did this occur because God was angry with us? No. It happened because Wichita Falls is uniquely situated in Tornado Alley. There is no need to read God's anger into this. Tornados occur regularly in Wichita Falls without the aid of God's emotions! Natural disasters are an outworking of the "great shop of power" (Emerson) as it is. They do not pummel upon us because God is mad at us.

I would do my best to walk away from a god who caused bad things to happen to me because of my sin. You can have that kind of god; I don't want any part of him. I believe God is my Friend, who does not cause bad things to happen to me but who is there to sustain me in the midst of my disasters!

I feel sorry for the sufferers who believe God is causing their pain, problems, or grief. They must relate to Him more like a witch doctor—with fear and manipulation—than as an Almighty Friend. God is not down on you, brother or sister. He is not the cause of your distress. He is not out to obliterate you because He is mad at you. He is your Friend, to whom you may come in any manner at anytime. He is committed to comfort and sustain you despite all of your anger and grief.

I struggled in my young pilgrimage with the fact that early biblical persons seemed to believe God punished individuals or nations because He was angry with them. I could not square this with my encounter with the God of the New Testament. I came to believe there are some ideas expressed early in biblical history that are later either fulfilled or abandoned. For instance, Abraham was a polygamist. The prophets, at a later date, hardly denounced polygamy. This does not mean Abraham was not God's man; he simply did not have the prophets' comprehension of the nature and character of God. One finds a more keenly developed moral sense in the prophets than the patriarchs. The earlier revelation of God was fulfilled by the latter.

I now see the ultimate and final revelation of God's feelings toward me in the life and teachings of Jesus. I believe He shows me what God is like. "God, after He spoke long ago to the fathers in the prophets in many portions and in many ways, in these last days has spoken to us in His Son" (Heb. 1:1-2). The Son's voluntary death has shown me that God has always loved me. "God, due to his constant love, takes initiative, breaks into man's hostility and throws down every barrier to an enduring and marvelous relationship."[4] He broke down the walls of separation, and enabled me to become His loving friend. My trials are not the result of His anger with me, but rather are an opportunity to discover His gracious help and love.

I have also discovered that sometimes I make bad choices and wrong decisions. This is like going the wrong way down a one-way street—the results can be devastating. There is no use to blame God for the corresponding grief associated with these decisions. I have made some occupational choices, for example, that cost me a lot of money. I could have sat around and said, "Why did God do this to me? Why is He causing me to suffer so?" The truth of the matter is that God didn't have anything to do with it. I made some choices for which we suffered; I am trying to be a man about it, take responsibility for it, and work out of it with God's help. I am certainly not going to blame God because I lost my shirt in a business deal.

Blaming God for the results of our own bad decisions is one way of trying to duck responsibility for our actions. We might as well grow up and try to take responsibility for the consequences of our decisions. For instance, the Israelites didn't believe God when He said they could enter the Promised Land. He did not just get mad at them for not entering. God ratified their decision not to enter the Promised Land. Their misfortune was the result of their bad decision. God's heart was broken over it. He gave them miracle after sustaining miracle until they could find the faith to inhabit the land. They were able to get on with their business only after they moved past the point of blaming God for the result of their mischoice.

Some times, though, bad things happen to us for no explicable reason. Karin's death is an example of this for me. We know of nothing during the course of Sally's pregnancy that "we" did wrong. We were not addicted to booze or nicotine. Somehow, Karin just developed a heart defect. We don't know why; it just happened. This is darkness covered in mystery.

I have a friend who is very ill for no apparent reason. She has no outstanding bad habits that would create the health problems she is experiencing. She is just sick. Why? I don't have the foggiest notion. I wish I did; I would try to stop her suffering. But I am helpless. I only know it's not God's fault and it's not her fault. It's just part of the incredible agony we live in every day.

I don't feel the need to place blame anymore or to try to be as smart as God. There is no way to get around having to live by faith. Life without darkened images and distorted reflections is heaven, and I ain't there yet!

I have found comfort in the solace of God. My friendship with Him has grown stronger through the years. Through all of the murky silhouettes of ease and comfort, erased in the struggle with the reality of life, I am encouraged by God's overwhelming and eternal love.

I hope and pray that myself, my friend and her family, and you, too, can continue to discover God is our Friend even in our pain, exhaustion, and sorrow. He will hear us and sustain us when everyone else on earth has lost the power or the inclination to care.

Notes

1. Reinhold Niebuhr, *The Nature and Destiny of Man* (New York: Scribner, 1943), 1:153.

2. Gustaf Aulen, *The Faith of the Christian Church* (Philadelphia: Fortress Press, 1960), p. 199.

3. The Old Testament concept of God's wrath is fulfilled in the New Testament message. Your concordance will give you both Old and New Testament references to the word *wrath*. The major New Testament references are: Romans 1:18; 2:5; 2:8; 3:5; 4:15; 5:9; 9:22; 12:19; Ephesians 2:3; 5:6; Colossians 3:6; and 1 Thessalonians 1:10; 5:9. Revelation, written in symbolic style, also contains some references to God's wrath. They are not, in my judgment, helpful in discussing the theological meaning of the term.

4. William Wilson Stevens, *Doctrines of the Christian Religion* (Grand Rapids: Eerdmans Publishing Co., 1967), p. 241.

4
Vocational Jitters and the Freedom to Decide

I have been a restless soul ever since I first began to seriously consider where I could be the most useful to God and the world. Carll Tucker identified this malady as creative imagination, or ideaphoria, and wrote that anyone stuck with it has a hard time holding a job! The gifts of the creative are more often a hindrance than a help he said.

> A student with an overabundance of ideas may find it hard to concentrate on routine schoolwork. High scorers [in ideaphoria] often shift from job to job, no one job satisfying their creative need. When Tolstoy said he'd have rather been a tree, he was regretting his high ideaphoria.[1]

I felt a strong feeling of call to preach when I was eighteen. Institutionally this call worked itself out as four years of youth ministry and seven and one-half years in the pastorate. Personally, the fire to tell my story has only increased over the years, even when I began to have doubts about my involvement in the pastorate.

I began to question whether this was the place for me at the end of my stint in Hamilton. I seriously considered leaving and entering law school. I decided instead to satiate my restlessness with involvement in the Doctor of

Ministry program at Southwestern. I accepted the call to City View at the end of my course work, did my project, and wrote my project report while pastor of that church. I worked there for three and one-half years, resigning in May of 1979.

So you ask, Did you make the right choice? I don't know; I have had ambivalent feelings about it for a long time. On the one hand, I faced the loss of much I held very dear. The special relationship of pastor and people was something I especially cherished. I loved most of the people of the church, and they loved me. I had many wonderful friendships and cordial relationships with almost everyone.

I played golf with Ron Clements, hunted quail with Ted Hoggard, ate Mexican food at the Pioneer Restaurant after church on Sunday nights with whomever would sit at the table, and played in some zany church league softball games with our team.

I remember the time I went belly flopping into third base, spraying dust and dirt all over the park, only to discover, after it had all cleared, that I was still six inches short of the base. Tommy Baker, our third base coach, was laughing so hard at me he nearly hyperventilated!

I also feared the loss of the proclamation of the gospel. I had lived to tell "the story." I still did, as a matter of fact. I did not know how I was going to exist without being a part of the forthtelling of the good news of Jesus Christ. I planned and worked toward a job that would still let me communicate some things about the gospel which were vitally important to me, but it fell through.

This meant I faced the decision to resign with a great deal of fear and trepidation. I felt I was doing the right thing, but I did not know for sure. I did not pack my books and sermons with celebration. I moved them slowly, almost regretfully, into their boxes.

On the other hand, I knew, if I were going to be honest with myself and with the people of City View, I had to go. I hated to go to work every day because there were aspects of the pastorate just as vital as preaching in which I was not interested. Maybe it was my idealism, but it seemed to me that if I were going to pastor I should love hospital visitation, outreach visitation, weddings, and funerals. I did not, and I have not since grieved over the loss of any of them.

I don't know why I felt a pastor should be committed to these things; I knew some who weren't. One accountant really shocked me into this reality shortly after I resigned. We were sitting around the Y talking after a workout one day, and he said, "Hey, I heard you resigned from your church the other day." I replied that I had, indeed. He asked me why, and I told him the honest truth: "I don't like it." The accountant's response got my attention: "Who does? My preacher doesn't like to pastor either. Now, he wants to be on TV everywhere, but he does not want to pastor."

The caving in of the job on which I had planned after I left City View did not add certitude to my decision. Neither did my subsequent vocational struggle and my growing grief over not getting to communicate the things which were important to me.

I have wondered, therefore, if I did the right thing in resigning. I have thought maybe the pastorate wasn't such a bad place after all. However, I believe the struggle has been worth the effort. I have sought to discover and use my gifts for God's glory with a singularity of mind I might not have mustered if I had been bogged down in the particular concerns of the vocational ministry. For example, I might not have written this book, and if I had, the whole story line would have been diffcrent!

Many things about the pastoral ministry caused me discomfort. I was and am all tied into doing something above and beyond the ministry of presence, and many times the primary ministry of the pastor is to simply be there. This is why I hated hospital visitation and funerals. I could not effect any change, and I felt like an impotent outsider. I only liked to visit when I could *accomplish* something. Just to go see someone to make a "pastoral call" drove me crazy! I spent about two hours every day running and clowning with the "perverts" (oilmen, lawyers, etc.) down at the Y, but beyond this I didn't really care about seeing anyone.

The flip side of this is that I felt limited in the interpretation and communication of the gospel by the pastoral duties to which I've alluded. I know this sounds funny at first, but think about it. I could not spend full time interpreting and transmitting the good news because of the need to do administration, counseling, and visitation of every kind. For instance, I had difficulty getting ready to preach because I felt guilty about studying. This was where my interest lay, however.

I had other concerns about my place in the institutional church which were instrumental in my leaving the pastorate. I think I was forced into the posture of trying to be concerned about every activity of the church, when I was not. I did not care, for instance, about having a charismatic, college choir in our fellowship just because someone else thought they were great. Try as I might, I just could not work up any enthusiasm for this, and I did not see why I had to show up. I did not even feel comfortable having them in our church, much less acting like I was happy to have them.

I could not have concern for every project. My idea was: "If you want to go to a meeting or function in which I am not interested, but which the church has claimed as its own, go ahead. But I'll be in the country with the dog, wife, and kids (unless the wife and kids didn't want to go, then it would just be me and the dog in the country)!"

Neither was I gifted for every activity of the church, and it was excruciating to act as if I were. Outreach visitation was an example: I abhorred it, but I had to be out front leading the visiting band because it was expected. Actually, the people who made such a stink over visitation usually never showed up for it. When they said, "We need to be more concerned about outreach in this church," they really meant: *"The preacher* needs to visit more." I always felt that if they were so concerned about visitation they should knock on someone's door in the dark. I was not into it.

I know, a bell just went off in your head, and you are thinking, *This guy does not care about the Christian faith.* Actually, nothing could be further from the truth. I am eaten up with the desire to be a part of the proclamation of the gospel. I would not have spent countless hours, days, months, and years on this book in the midst of two other full-time jobs if this were not so. I was just not gifted to knock on a total stranger's door about anything. I always felt like an intruder.

My problem with this kind of visitation, besides not being gifted for it, involved both its method and motivation. I am not sure, in our fast-paced society, that the old-fashioned, laid-back, door-to-door visit is welcome anymore by those outside the church. I know I cannot help but read my own feelings into this, but I don't want anyone knocking on my door unannounced at nine o'clock at night. I just want to be left alone with the precious little time I have with my family, and I will not be very nice if you show up to try to get me to do something I'm not sure about anyway! Many non-Christians feel the same way and need an approach that respects their time. The phone works just fine.

The other thing that bugged me about outreach visitation was that for a long time I could not understand for whom we were doing it. Was it for Jesus? If so, why were we so concerned that these people go to no other church but ours? Surely we weren't the only good church in town! Was it for us? If so, I understood this: Members and visitors alike were well served by being able to say they went to the church where things were really poppin', and I certainly could have used the raise which the income from more folk would have brought. But this seemed to be an awfully selfish motivation, and I could not fit it in with the spirit of Jesus.

This is why I lost my zest for being a great institutional church builder while still being concerned about the proclamation of the gospel. I was not convinced an honest call to the mission and ministry of Jesus would automatically translate into church growth. It seemed to me that it was easier for one who was so inclined to build a church, based on sound business principles (location, PR, advertising, and prospecting) than it was to preach a gospel that said, "It is easier for a camel to go through the eye of a needle, than for a rich man to enter the kingdom of God" (Matt. 19:24), or "Not every one who says to Me, 'Lord, Lord,' will enter the kingdom of heaven" (Matt. 7:21).

I was mindful that Jesus told it like it was and then

watched sadly as, on occasion, people walked away from
Him. I also thought about prophets like Jeremiah who
were called to preach coming destruction to a people who
only wanted to hear things were going to get bigger and
better. He was met with resounding apathy and abuse
and finally told God he wished he could just be quiet (Jer.
20:9) I am not saying the pastor whose church is not
growing is the only one telling the truth. I am saying that
if one is primarily motivated to build a kingdom the pastorate might not be the best place to be.

I finally decided outreach visitation was to show concern and care for the person being visited. Quaint, huh?
It's all I could come up with, and it seemed like an honor-
able motivation to me. I have simply decided I am gifted
to show care and concern some other way, like writing
books.

I used to get down on myself after I resigned the pastorate because I quit the logical place to proclaim the news
on which I constantly contemplated. It was very difficult
for me to serve in a particular locale, however, when I
was motivated to think beyond the local situation. A
great part of my consternation was that I wanted to go
beyond the four walls in which I found myself with the
message I preached. It was electrifying news, and I wanted everyone who had ears to hear to have that opportunity. This feeling of circumscription to a local area was
one of my biggest frustrations. I have decided that resigning from the local pastorate was not my attempt to dodge
the responsibility of preaching the gospel but was somehow an attempt to express my ministry beyond the four
walls of the local church in a way and place that was
appropriate for me.

It is easy to see from what I've written that I simply did

not fit my own image of who and what a pastor should be. Some parts of this image, like the deification of antiquated methods of doing church work, are ridiculous. Other things, like pastoral ministry, are critically important. I felt that since I was not motiviated or gifted in this area I should do the honest thing and seek to express my gifts in some other kind of ministry. Ultimately, I did not feel I was using my gifts and abilities to the fullest, and this is probably the reason I resigned. I just did not feel I was doing on a daily basis what I needed to be doing.

So I left City View, not knowing where I was going. I only knew there was something out there somewhere bidding me follow, and I had to proceed like a blind man in uncharted territory. I was in good company. "By faith Abraham, when he was called, obeyed by going out to a place which he was to receive for an inheritance; and he went out, *not knowing where he was going*. By faith he lived as an alien in the land of promise, . . . he was looking for the city . . . whose architect and builder is God" (Heb. 11:8-10, author's italics). This gave me confidence to proceed down the (bump!) road.

Many people simply wrote me off after I resigned from City View though. They voiced their opinions: "He doesn't care about the gospel anymore"; "He is running from God"; "He has turned his back on God"; "He is sinning greatly, and God will get him"; "He is turning into a reprobate and will end up in an insane asylum reserved for crazies and drunks." You get the idea. These people will be very surprised to hear that I am still alive and that I continue to believe. They thought I was a goner.

In fact, my relationship with the Lord Jesus, whom I had come to know as a forgiving Boss big enough to correct my mistakes, gave me the courage to resign from the pastorate. I was assured I was forgiven, even if I were making a mistake in the process. I had the conviction God would still be with me in the journey, even if I took an occasional excursionary detour off the main road. I believed I could make a mid-course correction and start again if need be. God was not going to condemn me to oblivion just because I missed a turn!

I found grace to begin again and hope to keep chugging down the myriad side streets of life by the assurance of this forgiveness. I believe faith in the forgiving God is what frees all of us to live with the awesome burden and privileges of making tough decisions. Otherwise, we'd freeze up as tight as a burned-up engine!

Does fear you might have the freedom to make a possibly costly decision keep you from accepting God's gracious, limitless forgiveness? Grace is free, but it is not cheap. It costs you the illusion that you are OK simply because you never try to do anything.

I have often asked for something other than the freedom to make mistakes and God's presence. I would like a road without any chuckholes, dangers, or side streets. I am not going to get it, however, and maybe it's just as well. For example, my decision to leave the pastorate has moved me farther and farther away from clinging to the things which I understood and trusted and flung me into the black hole of occupational uncertainty with only the light of God. I have never loved any job, therefore, as much as I have Jesus, and this is good.

Today, even though I have still not found my occupational nitch, I believe I did the right thing. I am moving in the right direction, and out of the distance I hear the encouraging words, "He who has found his life shall lose it, and he who has lost his life for My sake shall find it" (Matt. 10:39).

Note

1. Carll Tucker, "The Village Voice," 3 Nov. 1975.

5
The Binding Freedom
of Forgiveness

I'm into sin. I don't mean I enjoy sinning; I mean I take it seriously. As for myself, I have developed sinning into a fine art. I don't tamper with the grosser physical sins like adultery or child molesting. I concentrate on the sedate and seductive sins of the spirit, like bitterness, wrath, and false piety. I like these sins. All religious people seem to have them and, therefore, easily excuse them. We can then point a finger at the sinfulness of persons who take their sins on the physical side.

Actually, all sin is serious. It cost Christ's life. It has caused me a great deal of sorrow and grief, even as a Christian. I am never going to be perfect, and my sins are always before me—at times driving me to the precarious edge of desperation. I have, in times past, not been sure about my forgiveness. I used to keep asking God to forgive me, as if He did not when I asked Him the first time! It is in the face of the overwhelming nature of my sinfulness, in uncertainty about hard decisions I have made, and because of my drastic need for daily fellowship with God, that the good news of forgiveness has become something other than a cliche for me. As I have written, my decision to leave the pastorate was an experience in which I had to depend on the reflection of God's grace in forgiveness because I was not at all sure I was doing the right thing. I either made one of the headiest decisions I have ever made or I will one day regret what I have done. I *think* I made the right decision, but I do not *know* yet. Time will tell, and that is why in the meantime the forgiveness of God is so important to me.

I do know I have endured as much pain over trying to decide what I want to do when I grow up as anything else I have experienced. This grief over not being settled into something to which I am really committed is my most acute hurt now because it is as close to me as my next breath. It is there when I wake up in the morning.

I guess it is truthful to say I feel like a great failure. I feel I failed in the pastorate because I was not happy in it, and I feel I have failed out of the pastorate because I have not been happy out of it. I have had six jobs since May of 1980, four of which were jammed into a nine-month period in 1980 and 1981. As you can see, I have been extremely stable since 1981, having held only two jobs since then!

So how does this make me feel? Terrible, just terrible. How have I handled it? Sometimes, when I realize my family and I are still pulling together all in one piece, I think I have done pretty well. At other times, the grief and the guilt over not being sure of my future, and of creating a tremendous amount of insecurity for my wife, is nearly more than I can stand. I can then only tell God that I am sorry where I have failed Him and my family and find forgiveness and hope in that confession.

I have wrestled with what it means to be forgiven in such an experience. The realities of my existence have constantly banged up against the biblical message. I wouldn't need forgiveness if I could earn it, yet I have

often persisted in the attitude that my forgiveness was
based on my sacrifice or performance. I had depended in
part on my pastoral performance to keep my forgiveness
intact. I had thought that if I studied enough, prayed
enough, visited enough, and took it all hard enough I
would earn God's forgiveness.

After Karin died, I began to realize I could not earn
forgiveness. I could then only sit in a big, old, overstuffed
chair in my study and cry. I felt I was letting God down
in the performance of my duties, and yet I found that He
still loved me. I was not condemned because I could not
function, and that kept me from being totally debilitated.
I began to learn that my forgiveness originated out of
God's nature, not out of my meritorious ability.

This applies to you too. Your forgiveness is also by
grace, and there is not a thing you can do to earn it. There
is not an offering you can make for it. "Now where there
is forgiveness of these things, there is no longer any offering for sin" (Heb. 10:18). You can even go to the darkest
parts of the earth and die for God, but you do not earn
forgiveness by it. This is the message of 1 Corinthians 13
where Paul listed some truly outstanding religious works
by which we might endeavor to put ourselves right with
God. He concluded that we could perform all these works
and they would amount to nothing. Why? Because performing works in an effort to manipulate God into loving
us is an indication we have not accepted God's grace.
Christian works, born out of love, are a response to God's
love which He shared with us long before we thought
about doing anything for Him.

I have also decided forgiveness is once for all. When I
prayed, "God forgive me of my sins" again and again, I
was indicating ignorance of the biblical truth I was for-

given. Why ask for forgiveness when I was already forgiven? This is to repeat a mistake the Israelites made when they trusted in their repeated sacrifices to accomplish their salvation. The writer of Hebrews told us this tactic was not appropriate: "For the Law, since it has only a shadow of the good things to come and not the very form of things, can never by the same sacrifices year by year, which they offer continually, make perfect those who draw near" (Heb. 10:1). Instead of accomplishing forgiveness, "In those sacrifices there is a reminder of sins year by year" (Heb. 10:3).

I can certainly identify with the pilgrimage of the Hebrews. A part of my sacrificial system was trying to ask God to forgive me of every single sin I had committed. I agonized over this liturgy because I was afraid God wouldn't hear me if I forgot to ask for forgiveness of even one sin. This was torture for me because I constantly worried about those sins I had forgotten to mention or about those wrongdoings which I didn't even recognize as sins. Then one day it began to dawn on me that I might be forgiven. What a revelation and joy! I began to see the reflection of God's grace which told me I was forgiven in the heart of God and not by my efforts.

I believe I am forgiven now for every sin I *have* committed or *am* committing or *will* commit because I cannot find a qualifier on forgiveness in the Scriptures. "In Him we have redemption through His blood, the forgiveness of our trespasses" (Eph. 1:7)—not future trespasses or past trespasses but *all* trespasses, once for all, because "God in Christ . . . *has forgiven you*" (Eph. 4:32). This is wonderful news for me because it helps me deal with the despair I feel over my sin. I find it a great encouragement to know

I am forgiven, even in the midst of the frailties of my own nature.

"Doesn't this free me to live a wreckless, wanton life?" you ask. No. Paul recognized the temptation of people to abuse the free grace of God which offered total forgiveness. The recognition of this temptation was sharpened in the challenge of people who clung to the Jewish law as a supplement to Christ for salvation. They charged Paul with propagating a doctrine that encouraged people to sin more since they received grace in the face of their sins. Paul responded to this accusation by writing: "Are we to continue in sin that grace might increase? May it never be! How shall we who died to sin still live in it" (Rom. 6:1-2)? Paul believed that, if a person had received the forgiveness of all sins from Almighty God, there would be an overwhelming love response impowered by the Holy Spirit. One would then struggle to be a lifelong follower of Jesus. I also found this true in my own experience.

Luther also faced the accusations that some persons would use forgiveness by grace as an excuse to live licentious lives. He recognized that the truth he preached could be distorted as an excuse to live wicked lives. He did not believe, however, that he should quit preaching the truth which comforted the poor souls who needed comfort just because some folk chose to distort that truth.

One of the reasons I have such a hard time accepting God's forgiveness is that it calls me to forgive myself. Being a legalist, like the Pharisees, is easier. All I have to do is cling to the standards of my society, support the modus operandi of my culture, and trust in my little program (my little interpretation of Scripture, the way my church says to do it, and say, "Why, I am doing the best I can"). I might have to live with a little self-condemnation this way, but that is OK because I can thereby justify my lack of love for God.

I have found I am often afraid of grace. I have feared it will make me some kind of religious fanatic, and I was right. It has bound me to the loving God who has so freely forgiven me. This is also the experience of many of my friends who have been detained in their frivolous journey by God's grace. He is the epicenter, radius, and diameter of their conversation and the One for whom to live is their consuming passion. Watch out! He is out to get you, and He will if you ever catch the gleam of the forgiveness in His eyes!

6
Guilt, Forgiveness, and Liberation Toward Personhood

I have decided we have numberless opportunities to blame ourselves for our mistakes and failures when we make hard decisions. Sally and I have spent many anxious moments over wondering how we are going to pay off the mountain of bills acquired as a result of my decision to leave the pastorate. The guilt over feeling like I caused all this has propelled me to look for grace anywhere and everywhere. I found it in Jesus Christ, whose grace for my guilt gives me the hope to keep chipping away.

Actually, my guilt was compounded in the first bloom of my discovery of God's limitless, timeless forgiveness by my belief I would never feel guilt again. That was a hard thing to integrate into my experience when the decisions I was making were creating the very tension and guilt I wasn't supposed to feel! I wrestled with guilt over feeling guilt for a number of years. I just knew that since I was forgiven I shouldn't feel guilty. Wrong! Paul Tournier said it well when he wrote, "What grace removes is not guilt, but condemnation."[1] But I had not read Tournier upon my discovery of forgiveness, and my own struggle about what to do with my guilt caused me real problems. To feel guilty about feeling guilty is terrible, so what I tried to do was act like I didn't feel guilt. But for me, trying to cover up guilt was like trying to cover up sin, since I always felt guilty when I sinned. This led me to try to ignore my sin because I felt guilty about it.

My effort to cover up or repress my guilt emotionally crushed me, however, and began to cause me to loose grip on the reality that I am a sinner. Paul Tournier might as well have been reading my mail and exposing it to public view when he wrote: "Those who think that conversion gives shelter from sin and guilt are grossly deceived, and fall into a repression of conscience."[2]

I am beginning to discover that I am a sinner who feels guilty about my sins and sinfulness even though I am forgiven. Life for me begins again when I acknowledge my sins, over which I feel remorse and guilt, to God. I can then accept God's forgiveness in that moment. I think this is a part of what Tournier meant when he wrote, "In His grace God receives all those who are ashamed."[3]

So then, my forgiveness did not mean an elimination of my guilt. Actually, God's grace, of which total, timeless forgiveness is a part, heightened my sense of guilt. This was great for me, though, because it gave me an opportunity to agree with God about my sins and sinfulness and find His grace and forgiveness. As I acknowleged my sins to God and accepted His forgiveness for them, I found fresh new experiences of grace. Tournier affirmed this: "We have both at the same time a sharp sense of guilt and a sharp awareness of grace."[4] I need this grace moment by moment, for I am simply a forgiven sinner. "I did not come to call the righteous, but sinners" (Matt. 9:13; Mark 2:17), Jesus said.

Whether my guilt is real or false doesn't matter in my acknowledgment of it to God. My subconscious does not know the difference. All I know is that I feel bad about something. I often cannot tell whether I have actually done badly or if I only feel badly. Either way, I feel guilty. Real guilt is an opportunity to acknowledge my sin to God and to accept God's forgiveness in that moment. False guilt is an opportunity to accept His grace and affirm my desire for His will to be done in my life. To me, this acknowledgment of guilt, either real or false, feels the same. In the acknowledgment of my guilt, some real and some false, I have found grace and the expansion of life.

I wrestled with two passages of Scripture which seemed to limit forgiveness, however, as I came to believe I was forgiven of all my sins. The first of these was the Model Prayer, in which Jesus taught the disciples to ask, "Forgive us our debts, as we forgive our debtors" (Matt. 6:12, KJV). The legalists pounded away at me with this verse and tried to tell me I was not forgiven of all my sins, but only those for which I asked for forgiveness on a momentary basis.

I bought that approach for a while because Jesus seemed to be limiting forgiveness to a moment in time. I remembered, however, that this prayer was given as a model before Jesus had died to usher in the New Covenant of grace.

Persons were not yet enabled to see that God offered them forgiveness instead of condemnation. Jesus was pointing the disciples to that possibility in the Model Prayer. After Jesus' death and resurrection, His disciples began to understand God offered forgiveness of all sins and proceeded to proclaim that forgiveness to the world. I came to believe I was one of those for whom Jesus died and took assurance in my own individual forgiveness.

This prayer also pointed me to another reason I have such a hard time accepting God's forgiveness. It summons me to forgive those who sin against me. I got some help for this understanding by the *New American Standard Version* of the Model Prayer: "forgive us our debts, as we also *have forgiven our debtors*" (Matt. 6:12, author's italics). The prayer states that if we do not forgive persons who sin against us the Father will not forgive us. I have come to believe the overall message of this prayer is that I will have a difficult time accepting God's forgiveness if I refuse to accept His forgiveness of other persons. "It is not that God will not forgive the unforgiving but that the unforgiving have shut themselves out of the relationship with God by refusing to be reconciled."[5]

For example, I resented laypersons who bucked me in what I thought was best for the church when I was a pastor. I had an especially hard time with those persons who wanted to use the church as simply another place to extend their leverage as some of the most powerful persons in the community. This is a pitiful excuse for involvement in the local church, and I wish I had had the courage to call their hands. I fouled up by not exposing their hypocrisy and allowed my justifiable rage to grow into something dark and sinister. I really began to like my resentment of these kinds of people and wanted to hug it to my chest. I found, however, that God's total, timeless, and limitless forgiveness of me called me to struggle to grow to forgive them.

The truth is this: Justifying my sins is easier than accepting the forgiveness which calls me to forgive others who are also less than perfect. I stand in need of the forgiveness of God which calls me to struggle in the practice of forgiving others. "Be kind to one another, tenderhearted, forgiving each other, *just as God in Christ also has forgiven you*" (Eph. 4:32, author's italics).

The parable of the prodigal son was an illustration for me that my attitude toward others would affect my ability to accept forgiveness. The elder son was bitter because the younger son, who had wasted his share of the family estate, was reinstated as a family member in good standing upon returning home. Their father even threw a huge "welcome home" party for him!

The Bible tells us that while most folk were having an uproariously good time at the welcome home party, the older son was outside, mad. Now think with me a minute. Did the father wish to exclude the elder son from the party? Of course not. Did the father not love the elder son anymore? Of course, he did. The elder son was not in fellowship with the persons in the party because he had not forgiven his brother and had not accepted the fact that their father had forgiven him.

I see a lot of myself in the elder son. I bet he was pretty bitter about his lot in life, and I have been too. I have worked earnestly trying to do my best and have not received any special commendation for it. I have not even found a job that will hold my interest!

I'm afraid I have let my anger and bitterness have long-term residual effects in my relationship with people and have held grudges or been mean to Sally and Ike when in my heart I wanted to let these bad feelings go. I am struggling to face the reality of my bitterness, to ask God to help me love and forgive my enemies, and to accept God's forgiveness for these sins in my personal relationships. This brings healing and hope through forgiveness to me.

The other verse which seems to limit God's forgiveness to a moment in time reads, "If we confess our sins, He is faithful and righteous to forgive us our sins and to cleanse us from all unrighteousness" (1 John 1:9). As long as I kept my attention focused on the blatant, external sins of my life, I had little difficulty believing I could earn God's up-to-date forgiveness by remembering to ask Him to forgive me of each sin I committed. I could pretty well list these and be proud that I was not like real, hard-core sinners. Only after Karin died and all my religious facade was ripped away did I come face-to-face with how much I hated God. I then began to realize that sin was a much more serious problem than drinking or smoking and that I could not eradicate it by asking God to forgive me of some external act which was only a symptom of a much deeper spiritual cancer.

I have continued to discover my need for God's grace in my struggle to grow to love the unlovely and in my bitterness over not being able to find my place in the sun. I am a sinner; there is no doubt about it. But the good news of the reflection of God's grace is that I am a forgiven sinner!

I do not believe 1 John 1:9 detracts from this forgiveness. I decided it must be interpreted in the context of its chapter, and the chapter in the context of the entire book to understand its meaning. Notice the personal pronouns in the introduction of chapter one: "What *we* have seen and heard *we* proclaim to you also, that *you* also may have fellowship with *us*" (v. 3, author's italics). John was introducing the letter to two different groups, believers and nonbelievers. He no longer made this contradistinction between the two groups in the next chapter. He started it by writing: "My little children."

This led me to the conclusion that the first chapter of 1 John is an editorial introduction in which John was making his subject known to non-Christians who might read his letter. He introduced Jesus; he, along with other

disciples, had heard Him and touched Him. Now they
were proclaiming Him. Simply put, he was writing to
non-Christians and telling them how to become Christians and was not limiting the believer's forgiveness to a
point in time.

Paul wrote with a similar purpose in Romans 10:9
where he said if you "confess with your mouth Jesus as
Lord, and believe in your heart that God raised Him from
the dead, you shall be saved." He was not creating a
liturgy I had to perform again and again to maintain my
relationship with Christ. He was simply stating the
Christian experience: We confess with our mouths and
believe in our hearts that Jesus is Lord. John was doing
the same thing in 1 John 1:9: He proclaimed the message
of Jesus and then told others if they wanted to share
fellowship with Christ to simply confess their sins and
accept God's forgiveness.

Another thing that was extremely helpful for me to
remember was that *confession* does not mean "to ask for"
forgiveness. It is the English word for the Greek literally
translated "to agree with," so to confess my sins means
to agree with God about them. I am struggling and praying about being honest about the weakness of my human
nature, out of which arise my sins, shortcomings, and
errors in judgment. I do not want to feel the need to cover
up my humanity behind a mask of invincibility. Learning
Christian humility would free me to live with the real
power of Christ in my life, instead of sputtering along
with the false power of my supposed strength.

I have grown nauseatingly tired of persons who carry
their authority with a false air of superiority. Their position itself, either in the work place or as a child of God,
carries its own authority. They don't have to be pompous.

It is very instructive to note that the greatest missionary of our faith was known simply as "Paul."

No one is fooled by pompousness or false transcendence. No one believes we never make mistakes, even if we have deluded ourselves into thinking so. The plastic person, with a face as if carved out of granite, makes a great statue but a lousy human being.

The forgiveness of God has freed me to face myself, warts and all. I often don't like what I see, but I do not have to cover up the fact I am a human out of fear that God won't like me. I can relax around Him, knowing He loves me despite the fact I am not perfect. I do make honest mistakes; I am deceitfully wicked. But God has forgiven me of both sincere errors and scheming sins.

I confess I am both good and bad, at one and the same time, but the reflection of God's grace assures me I am forgiven. This liberates me to live with the contradictions of my own humanity, to accept God's grace when I fall short after a good effort or when I willfully choose to do evil, to try to grow to be strong enough to be my honest self before others, and to affirm them in their pilgrimmage to come to grips with the fact they will always be less then perfect. This acceptance of God's grace in the reality of "thy nature's weakness" [Whittier] is what Lionel Whiston called "humanness with power" and is emancipation toward being a redeemed person.

Notes

1. Paul Tournier, *Guilt and Grace* (New York: Harper & Row, 1962), p. 160.
2. Ibid., p. 159.

3. Ibid., p. 116.

4. Ibid., p. 158.

5. William Hordern, *Living By Grace,* p. 81. (Philadelphia: The Westminster Press, 1975)

7
The Support of God in the Midst of the Pits

I taught Old and New Testament survey in Wayland Baptist University's Extension Program at Sheppard Air Force Base, worked in a friend's carpet cleaning business, and played lots of golf the summer after I resigned at City View. The schedule was easy and slow and a respite from the toil of care I had carried so long. I began to relax and to look to the future with hope.

I decided to sell real estate in Austin, Texas, after suffering a major disappointment in my job search at the end of that summer. I had written a prospectus for a major Baptist university (I still have a copy of it) in which I described a service I thought they needed to offer. The chief executive officer was impressed and invited me to see him. He told me my chances of being hired were very good, and his assistant assured me my chances were better than 50-50. I was on the losing end of this betting line, however, and was not employed by the university. They did create a job in their organization using the ideas from my prospectus, but they hired someone with more experience. Real estate sales was my alternative.

We sold our home in Wichita Falls, pocketed the $3,500 profit, which was every dime of working capital we had, and moved to Austin. I began selling houses and did very

well for the first three months. I thought I was on the way
to wealth and fame, but only two of the families who had
signed a contract could qualify for a loan after a catas-
trophic five-point rise in interest rates. This killed any
chance I had of making it in the business as I simply did
not have the financial cushion it took to endure the slow-
down in the real estate market. I went from the pent-
house to the poorhouse very quickly!

That fall we tried to live on the slightly over two thousand dollars in real estate commissions I earned plus
what was left of the equity from the sale of our home in
Wichita Falls. Most of it had been eaten up by moving
expenses, security and utility deposits, first month's rent,
and down payment on a new four-door car in which I
transported clients. All of our money was gone by December, and so nearly were we. We were desperate, destitute,
and flat-out busted. We were so poor we had to move in
with Sally's parents to be able to make it. This arrange-
ment required great personal sacrifice on their part, for
which I will always be grateful. It also required great
personal humiliation on our part: I was ashamed to be
walking the streets with a doctor's degree and no paying
job!

Looking back on all of this I am sure the favor of God
kept me going. Personal circumstances were about as
bleak as they could be. My part-time job as a laborer in
a chemical plant, and then as a jewelry salesman, added
little to my self-esteem. I was living on the precarious
edge of hopelessness. I am sure the knowledge that God
saw me as righteous, and as a favorite of His, was the
sustaining factor in my life. He believed in me, even when
I couldn't believe in myself and feared no one else did
either. "The voice which says, not merely, 'you may go,

you are let off your penalty,' but 'you may come; you are welcome into my love,' "[1] is extremely good news when one is down in the dumps and out of a job!

God graced me in this time with the understanding that I had His favor, despite the mess I was making of my life. The Bible assured me that God's love for me was based on His love expressed in the cross and resurrection and not on my ability to keep it all together. I found a prototype for my experience in Abraham who "believed God, and it was reckoned to him as righteousness" (Rom. 4:3, quoting Gen. 15:6). "Reckon" means "to be declared," so this verse could be translated, "Abraham believed God, and he was declared righteous." Abraham did not have to wait until he achieved a level of moral accomplishment before he received God's favor; it was his the instant he accepted it! And I did not have to wait until my occupational and financial lives were in shape to feel the love of God; He comforted, confirmed, and strengthened me right there in the midst of all the trash.

The truth of the matter is that none of us will ever be worthy of God's grace, even if we had an eternity to prepare! I would not have merited His favor if I would have made a million dollars the first year out of the pastorate! We are in His favor only because He chose to love us. This is what the Bible means when it says God "justifies the ungodly" (Rom. 4:5). His favor is for those who do not deserve it, and I am so glad!

I was certainly doomed if I was depending on the great success I made of myself for God's favor. I have never been in any situation that lent itself more directly to the destruction of my self-esteem than being thirty years old, having had ten years of vocational Christian experience, a lovely wife and two wonderful children, and still being such a poor provider that we had to move in with my in-laws. This was death dealing. I moved like a zombie in those days, lumbering through each moment with the appearance of life but not the power.

God reaffirmed me in this time with love and showed me that even though I had utterly failed in the eyes of the world, I was still His child. He, to my utter amazement, favored me with His grace even when I couldn't buy a penny of it!

The Bible is full of examples that convinced me God's unmerited favor was for me and all the rest of us unworthies. For instance, Jesus set free the Jewess caught in adultery even though the Law stated that she should be stoned to death. She had been brought to Him by religious leaders who hoped to obtain evidence that He condoned sin. He defused their explosive accusations by saying, "He who is without sin among you, let him be the first to throw a stone at her" (John 8:7). They dropped their stones and slowly walked away. Jesus had judged righteous men by helping them to see their sin while setting free a woman caught in the act of adultery!

I liked that because at times I needed release and freedom from the same awful guilt and shame of failure that she must have so often felt. The positive and affirming reality of such an experience is that I had the opportunity to trust in the reality of God's affirmation and care even when I was covered up with humiliation. God's love, you see, does not originate out of our accomplishment but out of His very nature as gracious God!

This may seem backward to us religious folk who work so hard at trying to be good enough for God, but it is the message from the life and teachings of Jesus. I ran into this truth again and again in my reading of the New

Testament. For instance, the parable of the prodigal son, in which it seems the wrong son received the right reward, is an illustration of the truth that God's grace is for the undeserving. The elder son was very responsible. He had slaved away on the family farm and had never received any special commendation for it.

On the other hand, the younger son showed no respectability at all. He only wanted to play and finally left the farm with his share of the estate to do his thing in the city. He became disgusted with himself after a period of time, however, when he realized he had wasted his money "with loose living" (Luke 15:13). Brokenhearted and destitute, he knew of just one thing to do: return home and beg his father for a job as a hired hand. He knew he could never be a son again.

I can identify with the younger son. I too found myself stripped of my identity (pastor), without the people who had always supported me (the church), and with nary a nickel to call my own. I had not wasted my money with dissipation, but what I had done was in some persons' minds even worse—I had left "the ministry." I am sure they thought I got what I deserved, but I didn't. I got God's total and absolute and lavish love!

My reception paralleled that of the younger son when he returned home. His father was waiting, not to condemn him but to restore him to full sonship!

> The father said to his slaves, "Quickly bring out the best robe and put it on him, and put a ring on his hand and sandals on his feet; and bring the fattened calf, kill it, and let us eat and be merry; for this son of mine was dead, and has come to life again; he was lost, and has been found" (Luke 15:22-24).

But outside the house, the elder brother was furious

when he discovered all this merrymaking over his younger brother's return. What had he ever done to deserve a
party? Nothing! Absolutely nothing! On the other hand,
the older brother faithfully served the wishes of his father and had never had a big party thrown in his honor.
It just did not seem fair, and he was so angry he refused
to go into the party.

I can identify with the elder son too. I have faithfully
tried to serve the wishes of my Father. I want to do His
will; I am nearly consumed by trying to do what He wants
me to do right now. I work for a respected institution. I
serve on the board of directors of the Central Texas Chapter of the March of Dimes and am a member of its executive committee. I also serve on the McLennan County
Association for Mental Health Board, am a member of
the advisory board of the Waco Center for Youth, and
serve as the chairman of its program committee. I coach
Little League baseball and serve as a member of my
church's university committee. I also preach and do as
many retreats as I am asked to do. I am as busy as any
little Pharisee ever was, and yet I believe I am loved by
God only because He chooses to love me.

It's easy to get so caught up in our business, and in our
quest for performance, that we start to think we have to
do these things for God to love us. This is what happened
to the elder son. He did not love his father because he felt
compelled to work to gain his father's favor.

This is a dead-end street with a stone wall at the end!
There is no way over or around the fact that God's grace
for us is based on His disposition and not our worthiness.
We miss out on all the fun in life if we do not somehow
discover this loving God. Jubilation in life is for those who
don't deserve it?

I know this is outlandish, but God has helped me when I was hopeless. I have to write it, and I have to give you one more illustration from the alluring stories of Jesus to show its true! In the parable of the landowners and his laborers, the owner had hired a group of laborers at 6:00 AM to do a day's work for a day's wage.[2] He then hired additional workers at 9:00 AM, noon, and 3:00 PM. His last group of field hands went to work at 5:00 PM, eleven hours after he had engaged the first group.

He called the wage earners together after they had finished work and paid them, "beginning with the last group to the first" (Matt. 20:8). The men who were the first to get paid had worked for only an hour and yet received a full day's wage. Those who had labored all day began to hope for more than a denarius, but that is all they were paid.

This seems totally unfair. They did deserve more money than the other groups. After all, they had "borne the burden and the scorching heat of the day" (Matt. 20:12). The landowner's decision to hire them and not their work, however, was the basis for their pay. Those who were hired late in the day also received their pay because of the owner's decision to hire them. They claimed their wage as a gift, however, because they knew they were not worthy of it. And that is the moral of the story: We are in God's favor solely because of His decision to bless us with His mercy. His grace is not earned, it is received!

I resist this, even as I write it, and I realize that the pride in me would still like to think I could do something to be worthy of God. Pride might be my major problem, and it is one of the things that has kept me from accepting God's free grace. I like to think there is something I can

do, and in that very thought comes the awesome alienation fueled by the shackles of my good efforts that only
grace can overcome.

Carlyle Marney wrote about watching his parishioners
trudging into church, all dolled up but with the burden
of the sham of their hypocritical goodness piled in upon
them in their wrinkled brows and angry expressions.
They were trying to be Christians, but some of them had
missed the awesome paradox of the gospel which says
that the only person who can be saved is he who holds out
no hope for himself! There is unmerited grace for those
who don't deserve it but judgment for those who think
they do. Perhaps this is what the Lord meant when He
said, "But many who are first, will be last; and the last,
first" (Mark 10:31).

Jesus spent a great amount of time trying to help righteous people see that they, like everyone else, did not
deserve God's mercy. He taught Simon the Pharisee this
lesson while they were eating in the courtyard of Simon's
home (Luke 7:36-50). A woman prostitute entered the
courtyard and stood at Jesus' feet where He was reclining
during the meal.[3] She was so overwhelmed with what she
knew of Him that she began to weep, wetting His feet
with her tears. She also kissed his feet repeatedly and
dried them with her hair. She ultimately anointed His
feet with costly perfumed ointment.

Simon was offended by this whole affair. He did not like
the woman's intrusion into what was supposed to be his
show, nor did he like Jesus' complicity with her. *Anyone
who does not know this woman is a sinner,* he reasoned,
cannot be a prophet. In reality, Jesus did know she was a
sinner but accepted her anyway! He responded to Simon's
unspoken criticism by saying, "A certain moneylender

had two debtors: one owed five hundred denarii, and the other fifty. When they were unable to repay, he graciously forgave them both. Which of them therefore will love him more?" (Luke 7:41-42) Simon answered, " 'I suppose the one whom he forgave more.' And He said to him, 'You have judged correctly' " (Luke 7:43).

Simon and the prostitute were perfect demonstrations of this truth. He was righteous according to the customs of his culture and felt no need for forgiveness. He, therefore, did not love Jesus, through whom he was offered release from his sins. He felt no obligation to God and was seperated from Him by spiritual pride.

I am afraid, prior to the forced disassembling of my world, that I was falling into Simon's trap. The pastorate was the perfect place to spend a great amount of time doing good and religious things by which to gain God's love. I sure was proud I was not like everyday people.

The prostitute knew she had broken the Law and did not deserve the love of Jesus. She responded to Jesus' unwarranted grace by the outflow of her own thankful affection for the favor she was shown.

I, too, have responded favorably to God's grace, after it slowly began to dawn on me that He loved me whether I was in the pits or if I was enjoying the finest of the fruit. I prefer the fruit, but my situation does not effect His steadfast love for me.

I discovered this through the occupational disasters I have mentioned in this chapter. It was all a very humbling experience—to realize that I couldn't buy a soft drink but that God loved me anyway. It destroyed the fabric of pride that said achievement and success made me worthy of God's mercy and left me rather naked accept for the armor of God. I have decided His armor is enough, however, because I have seen the reflection of God's grace in His abiding help.

Notes

1. Richard M. Horn, *Go Free!* (Downers Grove: Inter-Varsity Press, 1976), p. 21. Horn is quoting H.C.G. Moule, *Justification By Faith* (1903: reissued by Falcon Press, 1959), p. 5.

2. Matthew 20:1-16. The denarius, worth eighteen cents in silver, was equivalent to a day's wage.

3. Persons often used this kind of gathering to assemble at a teacher's home to receive instruction. Jesus, Simon, and the prostitute were probably not alone.

8
Friends with God and Friends with People

I had applied for a job at Southwestern Bell prior to going to work in the chemical plant. Sally went to work in December as a bank teller, and then I was hired as a salesperson in the jewelry store.

I also went to see a state representative during this grim time whom I met in the real estate business and whose parents were longtime friends of my parents. I asked him if he knew of a job in which I might earn enough to provide the bare necessities of life for me and my family. He gave me the name of a statewide association executive director who had been ill and who might need some help in the upcoming legislative session. I called him, and he was glad to hear from me. He had some heart problems and needed some help in tracking legislation through committee and watching its progress on the floor of the house and senate. I decided to take the job and started to work in January, knowing I would need another opportunity when the session adjourned at the end of May.

Just about the time the job as a legislative assistant began to draw to a close, my father-in-law sold his house (the one in which we all lived!) to accept the call to pastor in another town. The new owners were to take possession in the latter part of May, and I needed a better-paying job by then, so we could afford a place of our own. I was running out of time!

The Southwestern Bell recruiter called during this time and told me I had passed assessment and had been approved for hire as a first-line marketing account executive. He didn't know when he could offer me a job, however, because an opening had to first appear in the account executive training stream. My calls to him, and my own doubts as to whether I would get this job, became more frequent as the session began to draw to a close.

This time was really bizarre. I had been hired right off the street at a management level in a major corporation, yet it appeared I could not afford to wait on the job! My responsibility as a legislative assistant added to the strangeness of it all. I worked for a respected association with its office only a couple of blocks from the capitol and rubbed shoulders with important people every day. They didn't know I was busted and was living with my in-laws.

I had given up on the Southwestern Bell job and had decided to try to sell golf clubs for a local manufacturer when Sally found me at the capitol. The recruiter had called the house to offer me a job! I returned his call from a pay phone on the first floor of the capitol building with Sally standing breathlessly outside the phone booth! He tendered me a job as an associate account executive, effective immediately. We negotiated over salary: He offered me an amount; I agreed. I accepted the position on the spot.

I was very glad to have a paying job after the destitution of the previous months. The saving grace of selling telephone equipment enabled me to provide for my family. My desire to speak for God in some capacity continued to gnaw away at me, however, and my years with the telephone company, although fruitful and productive, were not filled with the conviction that I had found my occupational home. I did not tie myself to the permanent hitching post outside the office at 712 East Huntland Drive in Austin, Texas, despite the fact it was a nice neighborhood!

I had a lot of frustration and anger in those years because I had not found my place in the workaday world, even though I had landed a good job with a lot of room for advancement. I hated myself because I couldn't be happy and settle down. We all wanted so desperately to settle down. I depended on God who was my Friend and of whom I was not afraid. I knew He could take the whole load, so I dumped it on Him.

I would not have made it had I not been able to express to my Friend every evil epitaph of bitterness and hatred I had toward Him in my frustration with how life was going for us. The thing I most wanted to do in life was to communicate the glory of what I felt about God, yet this was taken away from me when I could not function in the pastorate. I have not as yet found a job where I can unapologetically give myself 100 percent to this endeavor. Have I been angry? You bet! Am I frustrated? Constantly! I have found sanity and love for my family and friends in occupational disappointment only because I have been able to tell God exactly what I thought.

I remember a cold, clear night in Round Rock, Texas, when this was particularly true. It was one of those times when I didn't think I could go on—I was so tired of not being able to find a postpastorate vocation through which I could creatively live out my faith that I tore into God, hoping to make Him mad enough to do me away.

I was training for a marathon in those days, and I recall
running down the street waving my clenched right fist
toward the heavens and screaming at God. I was sick of
Him; I was sick of where I found myself; I was sick of
caring about wanting to talk about Him. I told Him I
hated Him and I hated His will. If He didn't like it, He
could just kill me.

He didn't, of course. I jogged on back to the house, took
a shower, went to bed, got up the next morning, and went
to work—business as usual. I did not find any of my external circumstances changed through that experience, but
I was amazed that God would let me talk to Him as I did.
I believed He would, but I was not sure. I became more
confident of His grace through these kinds of dreadfully
honest interchanges, however, and became more convinced than ever that He was my Friend.

God reaffirmed His friendship to me each time I blasted
away at Him because He listened to me, took my anger,
challenged me to love my family, and comforted me over
and over again. He never left me; He was bonded to me
in the commitment of His friendship.

My journey is, therefore, founded in the security to
wrestle with God, out of which comes the chance to better
get to know Him and what He's up to in the world. This
is a dynamic experience in which I find God accepts me
as I am in boldfaced honesty, but through which I am
never the same!

This is why I think that *the person who is not afraid to
question God about His purpose is the one who can live
most dynamically in the midst of the shadow and shade.*
This is the meaning of the parable of the sower, where
one of the types of soil in which the sower cast his seed
was infested with thorns. Jesus said the thorn-invaded

soil was like the lives of those "who have heard the Word, and the worries of the world, and the deceitfulness of riches, and the desires for other things enter in and choke the word, and it becomes unfruitful" (Mark 4:18-19).

"The worries of the world" are certainly realities for me, but I have found in my friendship with God the security to take to Him all of the things about which I am concerned. I have received fresh touches of God's grace when I have brought Him my unfulfilled dreams, shattered illusions, hatred, and bitterness. For me, God at least begins to weed out the thorns in such an open relationship.

The Lord Jesus found commitment to the cross only after a lengthy struggle in Gethsemane. He left Peter, James, and John three times to agonize in prayer over what lay in front of Him. Jesus' commitment was not without pain and honest distress. He was buffeted by the idea of dying the death of a convicted felon. He did not want to do it. He said to His disciples: "My soul is deeply grieved to the point of death" (Mark 14:34). He prayed, "Abba! Father! All things are possible for Thee; remove this cup from Me" (Mark 14:36). And yet He yearned to do the will of God: "Yet not what I will, but what Thou wilt" (Mark 14:36).

Jesus' struggle is typical of human experience. Those who think they are too mature to wrestle with God, or who say they have never questioned God, are either not honest with themselves or have not looked seriously into doing God's will. They are also placing themselves above the Savior, who found strength to act on His convictions only after a long, awful night.

Jeremiah and Paul are also examples of persons who endured and overcame trial because of the relationship they had with God. Their tasks were difficult. Jeremiah was called to prophesy war and the destruction of Jerusalem to a people who wanted only to hear of peace. To preach the message of devastation would incur their distrust and hatred.[1] He told God he was too young for such a job: "Alas, Lord God! Behold, I do not know how to speak,/Because I am a youth" (Jer. 1:6). God responded to him by saying, "Do not say, 'I am a youth,'/. . . ./Do not be afraid of them,/For I am with you to deliver you" (Jer. 1:7-8). Jeremiah found courage to fulfill God's call out of his communion and fellowship with God.

Paul found power to do God's will in the same kind of honest friendship with God. He did not think he could minister with his "thorn in the flesh." He asked God to remove it, but instead found strength in weakness:

> Concerning this [illness] I entreated the Lord three times that it might depart from me. And He said to me, "My grace is sufficient for you, for power is perfected in weakness." Most gladly, therefore, I will rather boast about my weaknesses, that the power of Christ may dwell in me (2 Cor. 12:8-9).

Paul found strength by "entreating" the God of whom he was not afraid. Paul's friendship with God was a catalyst for his ministry. Follow the example of Jesus, Jeremiah, and Paul—do not be afraid to enjoin God in the litigation out of which comes the passion "both to will and to work for His good pleasure" (Phil. 2:13).

Such an engaging friendship with Jesus has meant I want to grow to be like Him. I have wrestled with Him about His purpose, and now I am praying for Him to give me courage and strength to live in the world as a Christian, regardless of my circumstances. I need to have a job in which I find meaning and purpose, but if this does not happen, I still want to grow to be at least a little like Jesus. There is hope in this commitment because I know nothing can defeat it. Bad things will happen to me, but God can use them to help conform me to His image. I hope this means I am learning to love, without which I am a "noisy gong or a clanging cymbal" . . . or "nothing" (1 Cor. 13:1-2).

My love for others is best expressed as a reflection of the friendship I have with God. This means my friendship with Him can best be communicated to those outside my faith in the style of Christian kindness and friendship. Friends with God are friends with people. I am not free to adopt the I'll-love-the-sinner-but-hate-the-sin attitude if I really mean: I hate your sin, and I don't like you much either. I have known some Christians who have tried to justify this by rationalizing they are not under mandate to like the sinner, only to love him or her. This is an impossible distinction to make, however. I will grow to like the outsider if I truly love him. C. S. Lewis spoke to this point when he wrote:

> Though [Christian charity] is quite distinct from affection, yet it leads to affection. The wordly man treats certain people kindly because he "likes" them: the Christian, trying to treat everyone kindly, finds himself liking more and more people as he goes on.[2]

This quality of fellowship is potentially one of the church's most significant gifts to an impersonal society. I have seen this firsthand in the business world where concern for persons is often devoured by "the needs of the business." Lines of authority are long and complicated, and it is easy for the individual to be absorbed into the whole. The power of those in authority gives them the unfortunate opportunity to suppose they are superior to others. Insecure supervisors bolster their esteem by treating persons who work for them as objects.

The person who is kind to individuals in this environment is leaven in the flatness of psychic destitution. He is the light set on the hillside and the salt that has not lost its savor. He is a friend to whom others might turn to meet the Friend.

This growth in our friendship with God and others is not easy and does not happen overnight. I really think it takes an eternity. For me, it is not a destination at which I have arrived; it is a movable goal with which I occasionally make contact as I push it to new dimensions. I am like a dog nosing a ball all over the yard—frequently in contact with the goal but never quite grasping it! I love as I grow even though I often fail to love. I love, and then fail to love, only to love again.

This ability to begin loving again and again is my exciting hope created out of my friendship with Christ. He has assured me that He can work every trial and failure for the good of my being conformed to His image. This hope from my Friend enables me to grow in love, even in the very act of failing to love as often or as fervently as I would like. Perhaps this is a part of what Paul meant when he wrote:

> Therefore having been justified by faith, we have peace with God through our Lord Jesus Christ, through whom also we have obtained our introduction by faith into this grace in which we stand; and we . . . exult in our tribulations, knowing that tribulation brings about perseverance; and perseverance, proven character; and proven character, hope; and hope does not disappoint, because the love of God has been poured out within our hearts through the Holy Spirit who was given to us (Rom. 5:1-5).

Notes

1. Even Jeremiah's own family turned against him. They considered him a dangerous fanatic (see Jer. 12:6).

2. C. S. Lewis, *Mere Christianity* (New York: Macmillan Publishing Co., 1943), p. 117.

9
Facing the World in the Strength of the Lord

The Southwestern Bell job was the first one in which I had been compensated with a consistent and liveable wage since my time in the pastorate. I could actually afford to put Sally and the kids in a Waco apartment while I trained at a company facility in Dallas. We bought our own food, paid our own rent, and, on the weekends when I came home, went to the movies on our own money. It was heavenly.

I was suprised in a way that I got that job. My confidence, at the time of assessment and testing, was at a low ebb. My occupational turmoil and failures had left me devastated. I judged myself as having failed miserably in my vocational life and knew others had made a sport of trying to decide when old Steve was going to get it together. I had wondered myself, driving down Mopac Boulevard and ruminating in burned-out despair over whether I would ever find my place in the world. My attitude was in stark contrast to the beautiful hills around me, and it was a horrible feeling. Everyone else seemed to be so established.

I discovered through all of this, however, that I had strength in the weakness I abhored. The reality of my experience, wrenched from me by contention with God who would not let me get away, was that He loved me whether I amounted to anything. God's grace to me never wavered, even when I lost grasp of Him. I often screamed at Him to leave me alone; He never did. I began not to be afraid of appearing to be a failure because God had helped me in my enfeeblement.

This began to teach me my impotence and shame were in reality my vitality and dignity. I have come to be comfortable with my weakness because my infirmities are the fuel for the strength to serve. The weakness I so feared is actually the foundation for the strength of the Lord.

The New Testament affirmed this for me. Peter, writing to helpless little bands of persecuted Christians, encouraged them to "let those also who suffer according to the will of God entrust their souls to a faithful Creator in doing what is right" (1 Pet. 4:19), and to "humble yourselves, therefore, under the mighty hand of God, that He may exalt you at the proper time, casting all your anxiety upon Him, because He cares for you" (1 Pet. 5:6-7). I am sure this small, dispersed group of believers was not enthralled with the possibility of persecution and suffering. Peter would not have been so exhorting them if the specter of tribulation had been pleasing to them, yet they found in their need what it was like to trust in God and, in that trust, to find strength for servanthood.

Paul's discovery of God's strength in the epicenter of his own malady was a solace and encouragement to me because I had begun to discover that strength was not developed in the absence of weakness. The great apostle himself found his greatest strength in the midst of his greatest infirmities.

Concerning this [his "thorn in the flesh"] I entreated the Lord three times that it might depart from me. And He has said to me, "My grace is sufficient for you, for power is perfected in weakness." Most gladly, therefore, I will rather boast about my weaknesses, that the power of Christ may dwell in me. Therefore I am well content with weaknesses, with insults, with distresses, with persecutions, with difficulties, for Christ's sake; for *when I am weak, then I am strong,* (2 Cor. 12:8-10, author's italics).

I had read that passage, heard it preached, and even preached it myself ("Many men owe the grandeur of their lives to their tremendous difficulties."—Spurgeon), but I had never lived it. The journey I have described gave me that opportunity, although it is still hard for me to internalize this strength-through-weakness message. I, just like you, am into keeping up the appearance of power and control and am not too sure I want to be a servant anyway!

The reality of God's strength to me in my infirmities is good news, however, because it helps me to deal with the condemnation I place on myself and receive from others for my perceived weaknesses and sins. I am tempted to succumb to the judgment which is such an intricate and vital part of this world's design for evil, but I have been encouraged by other Christians who have stood the test of the world's condemnation. For instance, the Christians in El Salvador and Nicaragua minister despite the fact their motives and activities are under the constant scrutiny of political forces on both the right and the left.

The kind of strength they display in spite of the condemnation of opposition and suffering is found in the words of Juanita de Agila, when she discussed the killing of her husband, Mario, by guerrilas in El Salvador: "When Mario was here, I knew the Lord. He was at my side. But now the Lord is not at my side; he is inside."[1]

She goes on despite incredible pressure because she is convinced she is in God's favor, regardless of her circumstances.

The condemnation these Central American Christians face is more overt and direct than that with which I live, but it may not be as devastating for their Christian witness as the condemnation and fear which have been so much a part of my life. Yesterday and today I fear I am never going to be able to use my best gifts for God's glory, and I condemn myself for worrying about such trivial matters when there is a living to be made and a family for which to provide! I also find it hard to be meek in a society that worships power or to struggle to learn what it means to be a steward of my possessions when the judgment of the world tells me I am a success only if I collect a lot of money and things.

My fear of the condemnation of others is especially focused in the difficulty I have sharing my true feelings or convictions, which have changed and grown over the years. It is a scary thing for me to be cut loose from the anchors of the past to reach out to the trapeze bars of the future, but it is equally as hard to find the courage to express my new convictions or feelings. Nevertheless, growth is the normal pattern of life and has been fueled for me by the assurance of God's care and concern. This has given me some sense of security out of which I struggle to grow to be transparent about what I believe, without being controlled by the fear of what everyone else says or thinks about me.

Giving expression to my ideas and convictions is important for me. Perhaps this is why overcoming the fear of the judgment of other people is so consequential for me and is why I struggle to remember God has not given me

a "spirit of timidity, but of power and love and discipline"
(2 Tim. 1:7). This attitude is essential for me because it
motivates me to serve God, "not by way of eye service, as
men-pleasers, but as slaves of Christ, doing the will of God
from the heart" (Eph. 6:6).

I cannot be an effective person for Christ if I am dominated by the fear of other persons' judgment. The virtue
of Christian courage is essential for me to have genuine
interpersonal relationships and to live with grace and
power in a judmental world. I can only love folk (This is
my goal.) if I follow the great and practical advice of
Peter: "Do not fear their intimidation, and do not be
troubled, . . . being ready to make a defense to everyone
who asks you to give an account for the hope that is in
you, yet with gentleness and reverance" (1 Pet. 3:14-15).

This style of relationship is what I call "tough-minded
vulnerability" and is what it means to live out the acceptance of God in fellowship with friends and family. For
example, the growth of my closest friendships have been
as each of us, somewhat tentatively at first, began to
gingerly share what each of us really felt. Now I do not
fear my best friends, and ah, the times we have had
together! I recall the moments with Steve Simpler in the
special ambience of trees and greenery at Bob and Micha-
els, downing soft drinks and commiserating about life. Or
the times the Edwardses (Jud and Sherry) and the Lees
(Steve and Sally) have set up in the Edwards's family
room until the wee hours of the morning, drinking coffee
and talking about mundane matters like God, the church,
vocation, purpose and meaning in life, pain, sorrow, joy,
and family.

The times for these rendezvous are never often or long
enough. I have gained untold strength and support from

these people whom I can trust to be honest with me, without being judgmental or condemnatory. Our fellowship of ideas, convictions, sorrows, and joys is one of the things I would put at the top of the Most-Important-to-Me List and is a downpayment on the unconditional acceptance of Almighty God.

I have also found this kind of comfort in the support and open-ended love of my wife. She has hung with me through all of the grief and occupational turmoil I have described. Not many ladies would have done this, and the unmerited favor of God has been at least partially reflected in Sally's love.

Our marriage is not perfect; no one's is. We joked about my dedicating this book to her because we know of several authors who were divorced after dedicating a book to their respective spouses! We are both committed to the labor of keeping our relationship growing, however, and trust this will help us when the way gets dreary. I believe we must all be prepared for the hard work of maintaining and growing our marriage relationships or we may give up too early on the best place on earth to learn to reflect God's grace.

The growth and change of my own life was the context in which I began to discover the labor of marriage. I was one kind of person when we married: very sure about God, His purposes, and everything else. There was not much mystery involved in my thinking: I was sure with the brazen certitude of youth.

But after our world blew apart, I began to become a different person; that was scary. I mean, Sally knew who I used to be, but she did not know who I was becoming, and I was afraid to tell her for fear she would not or could not understand. I was also angry about the way things were coming undone, but I often failed to communicate it to her for fear she wouldn't think it was right.

Anger and negative feelings had been associated in my mind with sin, so instead of constructively expressing anger at some action or event, I drove it underground where it metamorphosed into nastiness. I knew this would not work when this cesspool of bitterness overflowed onto my family. I did not like or want this, so I had to begin to direct my anger and negative feelings at the events and actions which caused them, rather than into my caldron of criticism.

I have learned to express anger or disappointment at a family member's action, at my own inability to get something done, or at some circumstance I do not like. This is better than trying to suffocate my negative emotions because, once I express them, they are on the way to being gone. If I don't express them at their causes, for fear it is not "right" to feel that way, they resurface later as personal criticism and nagging, and my family does not need that from me.

I had to overcome the fear of the judgment that I was "sinning" when I expressed anger or negative feelings to begin to distill the criticalness which they had become. I believe anger, in and of itself, is a neutral emotion—it is neither good or bad. Expressing anger at specific actions or circumstances is more Christian than allowing anger to grow into a mean and hateful spirit. I know it is better for Sally and the kids, and what is best for our relationships is my heart's desire.

I believe, therefore, that beginning to overcome my fear of judgment, either self-imposed or from others, has helped me to begin to grow to win out over my tendency toward a critical and bitter spirit. I believe it has also helped me to begin to be a better communicator with Sally. I am on the borderline between an introvert-extrovert, and to succumb to the fear that Sally was not going to accept and affirm everything I said drove me into silence. I talked to her very little during those times because I was afraid she wouldn't approve of me.

We began to grow closer together than ever before, though, after I began to express my real feelings. They were not always pretty, and they may have begun to lead us in a new direction, but having the courage to speak my piece helped me to feel better about myself in the down times and made me a more animated, whole husband rather than just a hunk of meat who slept at home.

Of course, and absolutely, this is a two-way street—Sally has the same freedom and right to tell me what's on her mind and to disagree with me, as I do with her. She is a growing child of God also and will grow to overcome whatever fear she might have of my considered and unconsidered opinions.

I am glad she has found the strength to do this because it means that she is maturing in her own self-esteem and that my criticalness has not gotten her down. I am most grateful for this because the way has been long and hard for me, and one of my greatest fears was that I was going to tear us apart before the image of God's love was built into my attitude and spirit. Praise His name, He has continued to be more committed to our relationship than even we are. This is because He is bonded to each of us as His individual child. We have found stability in our fluid, boundless, changing, and dynamic fellowship because we have found this same commitment to each other as Christians. We want to allow room for each other to grow and develop because we respect each other as persons in the family of God.

I am no expert on marriage, and I talk a much better game than I play, but Sally and I *have* made it through some times when our finite human love has been shrouded in the fog of our own pain. I am thrilled to discover that I am now more committed to her, Ike, and Andrea than ever before. The aloneness of being away from home for three of the last four weeks served as a poignant reminder of this for me. I was on the return trip when the thought struck me: *I am going home, and there is no better place for me!*

I also believe the fear which presses us to please people rather than God, and to lose our individuality and convictions, weakens the witness of the Christian community. This is important to me because the concerns of the Christian community are my concerns. The things I think about the most are matters that involve my own relationship with Christ and the kingdom of God.

The church is a big part of that interest, and I worry that we are in danger of being shaped by the pressures of culture, rather than speaking prophetically to culture's mad desire for money and power. Prophets have joined forces with politicians to present a unified front for acquiring and hording cars, money, buildings, budgets, and the illusion the faithful are secure in Zion.

Israel, in the time of Isaiah, abandoned her faith in God to form alliances with the "in" political power. My soul and conscience, which have been fed in following Christ in the darkness of despair and found strength in weakness, cries out no to all of this. I believe simple faith in Christ is the only power that will see us through. I will not be like the false prophets of Jeremiah's day who cried,

"Peace, peace" (Jer. 6:14) when there is no peace in the alliance of politics and religion. Civil religion is a cursory idol that is doomed to be destroyed and that is one example of how the church is acceding to the demands of our culture.

I am my own priest before God and I serve in a local church which is autonomous in its own belief and practice. I willfully choose to cooperate with other Christians who do not believe like me at every point so that we may further our witness and ministry. I refuse to buckle under to those who set themselves up as God's watchdogs. God does not need a watchdog, bless His name!

The fear of judgment also enfeebles the ability of the free church to articulate its mission to the world because it deters the open and frank discussion out of which the church defines itself. I'm afraid my silence, far from being a desire to keep peace in the church, has been a gutless acquiescence to the fear others won't like me because of some of my ideas. Let me give you an example: We laid new carpet in the auditorium of our church building when I pastored in Hamilton. The choice of colors came down to blue or rust. I hated the blue but didn't come right out and say it. I, instead, entered into an esoteric monologue about the color of God, hoping everyone must know His character was symbolized by rust instead of blue. Other persons did not say a word about their perference. They voted to buy the blue carpet, despite the fact they didn't like it. They were trying to humor their young pastor whom they thought wanted blue—the sky is blue, you know! I didn't tell them what I wanted, and they didn't tell me what they wanted, so we all decided to buy what none of us wanted!

This is a reminder to us that we must not let the fear

of fellow church members deter us from speaking our piece in the church. We can only relate our mission to the community if we know what it is. We can only know what it is if we define it through open and honest communication.

I have always been frustrated by the persons in church who really wanted to say something, but let their fear of other people's judgment control their ability to speak out. This was especially true for me when I was in the pastorate because no one was as likely to disrupt "the communion of the saints" as the person who was afraid to state his convictions in an open forum. He sat silently in a protracted business meeting in which a decision was made with which he did not agree, only to return at the next session with three or four malcontents to raise a ruckus over what had been democratically decided! Why didn't he state his opinions in the first place? Because he was afraid to speak for himself; he had to first raise the support of other fearful individuals.

I do not like to see this happen, and I wish everyone felt the freedom to honestly state their own convictions in an open forum. This is the way to vent frustrations or concerns without distilling them into a bubbling caldron of bitterness and hate. Clear the air in honest discussion about God's work and communion will be sweeter.

I have also reflected upon my work in the business world as it has been effected by my fear of other persons' condemnation, and I am convinced the fear of judgment gums up the works and hinders my productivity as well as that of others. I am no business consultant or efficiency expert, but I want to reflect on this. You business persons bear with me. I cannot help but do this since my faith touches everything that touches me!

I have observed the curious practice of some who spend more time whispering to the person in the next desk or office than working, trying to determine whether everyone else in the building was pleased with them on mostly inconsequential matters. They then spent most of the remainder of their time worrying about something that had already happened or preparing to meet everyone's future expectations, whether they were justified or not.

This kind of stuff is counterproductive, at least for me. I am aware there are those who are followers, who work best when they are exactly in step with what others want. These people make the best torso of any organization, but every body needs appendages who are willing and able to move the torso along. I guess I must be an appendage-type person because I get a lot more accomplished when I am leading or, if I must serve down the pecking order for an institution, when I am given the freedom to do my own thing. I find I do this anyway, and any structure which leans on my individuality or leadership skills won't have me around very long.

This means the organization or business which tries to motivate me by fear might as well try some other technique. This crushes my creativity and energy, and the work I am doing for them will not be as effective as if I were told what to do and then left alone. I believe any business that is in the growth cycle of its life needs to award individuals for their initiative and creativity, and management needs basically to stay out of the doers' way. Perhaps a stale and stagnant establishment, content to try to stay alive in the crush of competition, can exist on fear but not the one which is dynamically meeting the challenges of its environment.

I recently read an article from a friend's church newsletter, in which he wrote about some research on creativity he had seen, which bears this out. Researchers have discovered that creativity diminishes when one's goals are imposed on them by others or when they are pressed by fear of firing or lust for money. The findings also showed that the greatest single boon to creativity is freedom. My buddy wrote, "Those people who have the power to decide what to do and how to do it are most prone to strike the innovative spark."[2]

Sadly, many organizations suffer the disease of conventionality and form, which is driven by the lust for power of those in authority. This destroys the creativity which could help the organization meet challenges. "There are pressures in our society to conform, to go along. Einstein said what a genius needs most is just freedom to pursue. Generally our system is designed to be adverse to that."[3]

I guess what concerns me most about the way fear, judgment, and authority are used by institutions, and why I have written about it in a book about my personal Christian pilgrimage, is that I think it's sad to see individuals crushed by institutions. Maybe this is because I'm a maverick, but I think not. Jesus died for individuals, you see, not buildings or organizations. I have never read where it says, "For God so loved the business . . ." It just seems to me that Christian business leaders have a responsibility to be different in the way they treat the people who work for them. The person wins out with Jesus every time over the business, organization, or institution.

Maybe that is the bottom line to this chapter: Jesus sees each of us as important individuals, and we really are precious in His sight. We do not need to fear our weaknesses or uniqueness, for in our infirmities we find strength to love folk.

We can all take heart in the favor of loving God and live out of this reality, not out of fear. We have been declared not guilty before the judgment seat of Almighty God and welcomed into God's favor. The power of these realities is greater than any human judgment as we struggle to be authentic Christians in a pagan age. The favor of God is good news, therefore, not only because of what it tells us about our relationship with Him but also because it encourages us to carry out our right standing with Him into the judgmental relationships of the world.

> Who will bring a charge against God's elect? God is the one who justifies; who is the one who condemns? Christ Jesus is He who died, yes, rather who was raised, who is at the right hand of God, who also intercedes for us. Who shall separate us from the love of Christ? Shall tribulation, or distress, or persecution, or famine, or nakedness, or peril, or sword? But in all these things we overwhelmingly conquer through Him who loved us" (Rom. 8:33-35,37).

Notes

1. "The Commission," Oct.-Nov. 1984, p. 26, Foreign Mission Board of the Southern Baptist Convention, Richmond, Va.

2. Newsletter, Heritage Park Baptist Church, pastor's column, 12 Feb. 1985.

3. Ibid., quote from Dean Keith Simonton, *Genius, Creativity, and Leadership*.

10
Journey on the Road Toward Servanthood

I worked for Southwestern Bell for three and one-half years, and I think I did a good job for them. My boss, before I turned in my resignation, told me I was a good account executive with the potential to be a great one. But what is the saying? *Potential* is one of the most burdensome words in the USA! One can only have potential for so long. I knew this, and not being willing to settle for good if great were the possibility for a job in which I was interested, I began to surreptitiously look for another one.

I found it as the director of development for Hillcrest Baptist Medical Center in Waco. This is the very institution in which Karin struggled for her life for three months, prior to her surgery in Houston. Not many people in the hospital know about her, and the silent irony of working in the place in which my daughter waged a losing battle against death is always with me. I have been in the pediatric unit several times, and it is always a strange experience. I walk into the very room in which she slept to visit patients.

This reflection on my own pain reminds me of how Karin's death has helped me to begin to see God's love for other wounded persons. I have begun to mine the depths of His love for the hurting in the fragility of my own spirit. Because of the love He has for me in my sorrows, I know He cares about others in their weakness.

This growing concern for individuals is the meaning of the Christian life for me and is accurately reflected in the life of Jesus who "did not come to be served, but to serve" (Matt. 20:28). Jesus' concept of life as servanthood was indeliby portrayed when He washed the disciples' feet (John 13:1-17)—a task so menial "even Jewish slaves were not required to perform [it]."[1] His disciples had been squabbling over who was the greatest among them.[2] Jesus, upset with these kinds of attitudes, "rose from supper, and laid aside His garments; . . . and began to wash the disciples' feet, and to wipe them with the towel with which he was girded" (John 13:4-5). He then said, "If I then, the Lord and the Teacher, washed your feet, you also ought to wash one another's feet. For I gave you an example that you also should do as I did to you" (John 13:14-15). His message is clear: The life that is most in tune with His Spirit is the life of servanthood.

The big question for me, therefore, is: Am I becoming a servant of Jesus and of every living person? The answer is that if I am it often goes undetected by me and everyone around me! Seriously, I have barely begun to live out God's care for individuals, but I believe this is the goal toward which God is working in my life. I often do not recognize God's labor, but His promise is that He is moving undeterred to make me a lover of persons, even though at times the progress is almost imperceptible. Maybe this is the reason for eternity!

There are many conterfeits to the goal of servanthood in our day, and I believe I have fallen for everyone of them! I have been tempted to succumb to the idea that the accomplishment of riches, power, and achievement are the primary things in life. I was encouraged to make riches primary by a theology which says, "It is God's will for you to prosper." I saw God, in this perspective, not as the supreme Lord God Almighty but as a benevolent Santa Claus who had promised to dole out money to help me meet my financial goals. I was enticed to accept God's care and grace, not as a basis for service, but as the motivator in my search for things: "God loves you, Boy— now go get'em!" This is a far cry from the spirit of Jesus who sent the disciples into the world as "sheep in the midst of wolves" (Matt. 10:16).

I have seen this "prosperity theology" in practice in the motivational rallys I used to attend when I was a salesman. At one of these, a deacon from one of the largest churches in town prayed for everyone in attendance to be "successful" (rich). One speaker told us to hug everyone we met because we'd sell more if we did! It was easy to justify the manipulation of persons to accomplish this end since it was God's will for us to be wealthy.

The abuse of care and concern for others is what happens when sanctification is defined as the accumulation of wealth, but I don't believe God cares whether I am rich. There is a great chasm between my wants and needs anyway, and I have quit trying to prop up my desire for things by saying God wants, wills, me to have them! Wealth is incidental to God's will for my life, which is that I grow toward service.

I must confess that early in my short-lived but brilliant pastoral career (?!) I was more concerned about the appearance of success than about growing to be a servant. The human desire for power and worship of materialism was obvious in several of the things with which I wrestled and which I have observed in others. I think the concern that I had, and others have, with the size of programs and buildings in our local churches is worship of the idol of materialism. This is more a reflection of the successism of our culture than the will of God. It is especially true in the Bible Belt, where we mostly build buildings to house Christians who have joined from someone else's church. It seems to me that if we were truly concerned about reaching the unchurched we would always keep mission giving as the top priority in our churchs' budgets.

I have not always had this perspective. For example, I led a church I pastored to reduce its mission giving by 5 percent to support one of our local programs, and I am sorry. I now feel that was a mistake on my part, and it was definitely not a reflection of the Spirit of Him who said: "For whoever wishes to save his life shall lose it; but whoever loses his life for My sake shall find it" (Matt. 16:25).

I now feel the fellowship which limits its mission gifts while building an edifice worth millions of dollars is sending a signal that new bricks and mortar are more important than service. So is the downtown church which leaves its field of ministry to the disinfranchised and moves into the suburbs to spend tens of millions of dollars to create a structure in which to house a mostly white, upwardly mobile congregation.

I also used to be more concerned about the numbers we had in Sunday worship than anything else related to the church. Now there is not a preacher alive who is not concerned about the number of people who are going to show up next Sunday, and there is certainly nothing wrong with large numbers of people coming to hear the gospel. But there is something wrong with letting our concern for numbers so consume us that we compromise what we preach to attract people to a cheap gospel.

I found it very hard to stay in the pastorate with these convictions, especially when the congregations in which I was interested were more concerned about whether their pastor was going to lead them to be a going enterprise rather than if he was going to lead them to ministry. I feel the church has exchanged servanthood for materialism when it is more concerned about drawing a crowd than ministering to the needs of people. We have only reinforced prejudices for materialism when our primary concern is the numbers we have in attendance. We must be careful not to proclaim the cheap successism which brings a lot of attractive people to worship services but does not challenge them to servanthood.

I used to respect only the pastors of big churches and wanted to be just like them. Now I'd settle for the spirit of my father-in-law and Daddy. My father-in-law, who died this year, was a faithful pastor for thirty-two years. He never pastored any of the large churches of his denomination. He labored in obscurity for most of his life. He was never asked to pray or preach at state conventions or any other large denominational gatherings. And yet I know of no man who was more Christian in most of his attitudes than Curtis Simpson. He was not perfect; he had his weaknesses just like the rest of us, and yet, at his funeral, the church house was packed with people whose lives he had touched. He was no big hero with a large television ministry flashing his face all over America; he was just a faithful servant of God who had gone quietly about his job for thirty-two years.

My dad, seventy-one years old now and still pastoring a little country church outside of Bertram, Texas, is a man I respect as much as anyone I know. He says he can't remember getting much early education and knows he didn't go past the third grade, and then only fitfully. He felt called to preach, though, so he, mother, and my brother and sister (I came later—surprise!) packed up and moved off to Brownwood, Texas, to enter college. Dad says the dean was rather incredulous he wanted higher education, having had little or no lower education! Dad also says there was no use to take the college entrance exam because he didn't know anything. This is not true, of course; he owned his own grocery store before he went to college. He was lacking in formal education, however.

Dad was once pastor of a church for eight years without a salary. He made a living as a butcher. The church then began paying him, and he stayed sixteen more years working as a butcher and as pastor. Dad's largest church averaged a little over two hundred in Sunday School. He then "retired," moved to Lake Buchannan, and began to pastor Mount Blanc Baptist Church. Again, he has made no big splash by his ministry; he was, and is, just God's man trying to do the best he can with what he has for Jesus' sake, and I love him very much.

My experience with these two men and others like them, along with my ideas about true greatness being found in a servant attitude, has led me to the conviction that the denomination which reveres as its leaders only the big personalities with the big churches, or the layperson whose primary qualification for leadership is the possession of money, is also in danger of falling prey to materialism. Worldliness reigns in the church when pastors who have served in the smaller places of service, often at great personal sacrifice, are humiliated and ignored because their congregations are not as large as others. The Christian enterprise is in real trouble when a pastor's worth is gauged by the size of his congregation. Nothing is more shameful for us than the disgrace of ministers who serve with dignity.

I guess you can tell I am now leery of the very thing I used to love: the complete "superchurch" syndrome. Sure, some churches have a lot of beautiful people in attendance, but I wonder for what—to be part of a booming business where the latest, strongest personality preaches, to compare their clothes to the fadful fashions of other people, to make the right business contacts, or to go where all the other yuppies go? Is this the reason God called them together as church? Is there not more to the body of Christ than the baptism of our culture and the certification of religion upon our mad dash toward materialism? Yes, God help us, there must be.

My pilgrimage has, therefore, led me to change my mind about what a "good" church is. I used to think it was only the one situated in a high-growth area of town (These were the ones that grew fast and would make me a "star."), or that it was one that had a lot of doctors and lawyers in it (These are the ones with money and would pay me well.). I guess all of these things are important, and there are plenty of needs in high-growth areas (single parents, family problems, alcohol and drug abuse), but one can be tempted to try to pastor one of these churches to accumulate power for oneself. I have now decided that what makes a "good" church is not where it's located or who goes there, but is rather a group of persons following Christ, trying to meet the needs of other people, especially hurting and needy people, wherever they are found.

This has led me to the conclusion the church has exchanged power for servanthood when it abandons its concerns for the weak and becomes simply another place of leverage for the strong. This happens when the gospel, in which "there is neither Jew nor Greek, there is neither slave nor free man, there is neither male nor female" (Gal. 3:28), is held hostage by the strong, white, male hands grasped tightly around its neck! It also happens when the mission of the Savior "to preach the gospel to the poor, . . . to proclaim release to the captives, . . . To set free those who are downtrodden" (Luke 4:18; Isa. 61:1) is throttled by the powerful who have chosen to ignore the words: "To the extent that you did it to one of these brethren of Mine, even the least of them, you did it to Me" (Matt. 25:40). A "good" church is not one, therefore, that accumulates power to itself just for power's sake but rather gives itself away to meet the particular needs of persons in its community.

My disposition for trying to acquire power has been found in the allure of trying to combine my Christian convictions with politics. I have been tempted, as one who wants to make an impact for God upon society, to try to encourage others to legislate what I think is right. But the very nature of Christianity is the free and uncoerced will one may exercise in his or her relationship to God. It is both bad for the state and bad for individuals if one is forced into the exercise of religion. It is bad for individuals because it leads to the neutering of personal faith in the name of religion, and it is bad politics because it leads to the crushing of human rights.

This is why I feel believers have succumbed to the desire for power when they ignore fundamental Christian liberties to justify their desire to control others and use political power to try to force their views on others. Pas-

tors and people become power brokers when they aban-
don the foolishness of the message preached for the wisdom of the world and trade the cross for the scepter. Such
Christians exchange the weakness through which
Christ's Spirit is revealed for the power of self-assertion
and evangelism accomplished by persuasion and conviction for external conformity accomplished by coersion
and conformity. Plenty of these people are in churches,
and they have sparked in me a renewed passion for essential religious freedoms!

I have always been an achievement-oriented person. I
am happiest when I am doing something and am most
gratified when I have done (as in, worked on and finished)
something. I write goals and make business plans. I have
a five-year career plan in my desk drawer right now toward which fulfillment I am working. However, I have
decided that achievement is not God. This was and is hard
for me. I bought into the spirit of the age which loudly
shouts, "Anything the mind of man can conceive, his will
can achieve!" I attended human engineering seminars
and read the precepts of the human potential movement.
The wonderful hope of human ingenuity combined with
the you-can-have-it-all mentality of our age has had the
magnetism to attract my attention. The hope of achievement and wealth, promised as the will of God for my life,
has been awfully alluring. But I have decided that my
boundless enthusiasm for my potential has been mis-
placed and that it needs to be tempered with the understanding it is potential for evil as well as good. I can do
a lot of things; I often fail to do what is right!

I am a part of a species that has invented great
technology and the weapons of absolute annihilation
and nuclear winter, air-conditioned homes and cars,

drunkenness in the living room and on the highways, colored TV and pitiful programming, home computers and machinelike persons, information systems which transmit both voice and data and people who can't communicate, electronic mail to faster dispatch bad news, genetic engineering and an epidemic of broken homes, the space shuttle and neighbors we don't know, and digital watches to remind us we are running out of time! We have also created a world with war and distrust among the nations, rampant world hunger in the midst of untold wealth, and superpowers grasping their knowledge and strength to themselves rather than sharing it with the broken and bleeding people of the world.

This hodgepodge of right and wrong, plenty and hunger, good and evil, righteousness and sin, and comedy and tragedy leads me to the conclusion, "The only ultimate disaster is to feel ourselves at home on this earth."[3] I am struggling, therefore, not to get caught up in the god of human achievement, but rather in God's purpose. I am beginning to see that I and others have not, and will not, arrive until we are ultimately and finally changed.

For my money, the Christians, the saints-who-are-sinners-on-pilgrimage, are growing toward servanthood when they incorporate basic concern and respect for every individual into their life-styles and are committed to personal human dignity. They will identify with every person in his or her need and with the Master's care for the powerless of society. They will stand with the weak against the strong and strive to perserve the dignity of the person against the power of the institution. Jesus gave an example in the life He lived and in the death He died to reflect the love of God for every individual. Who is going to be concerned about persons if those who claim to be Jesus' followers are not?

This kind of consideration for the individual is beautifully illustrated in "The Beloved Captain." It was said of the senior officer:

> We all knew instinctively that he was our superior—a man of finer fibre than ourselves. I suppose that was why he could be so humble without loss of dignity. For he was humble, too, if that is the right word, and I think it is. No trouble of ours was too small for him to attend to. When we started route marches, for instance, and our feet were blistered and sore, as they often were at first, you would have thought that they were his own feet from the trouble he took. Of course after the march there was always an inspection of feet. That is the routine. But with him it was no mere routine. He came into our room, and, if any one had a sore foot, he would kneel down on the floor and look at it as carefully as if he had been a doctor. Then he would prescribe, and the remedies were ready at hand, being borne by a sergeant. If a blister had to be lanced, he would very likely lance it himself there and then, so as to make sure it was done with a clean needle and that no dirt was allowed to get in. There was no affectation about this, no striving after effect. It was simply that he felt that our feet were pretty important, and that he knew that we were pretty careless. So he thought it best at the start to see to the matter himself. Nevertheless, there was in our eyes something almost religious about this care for our feet. It seemed to have a touch of Christ about it.[4]

My personal growth toward care for persons has led me toward certain commitments: I will not stereotype individuals or be sterotyped myself. I will fight for the freedom of individuals who do not believe like I do, which means I might be accused of condoning sin. I will oppose the powerful people's efforts to control and take advantage of the weak. I will stand against the Christian power broker's intention to force his faith on others. I will resist the authoritative effort of some to force their interpretation of things on others I will stand for Jesus Christ as the only criteria for the Christian faith. I will seriously try to do my part to minister to the poor, the helpless, and the needy of our society, and to starving persons around the globe. Now—I've said it! If it was only as easy to do as to speak.

Notes

1. Malcolm O. Tolbert and William E. Hull, "Luke-John" in *The Broadman Bible Commentary* (Nashville: Broadman Press, 1970), 9:328.

2. This detail is given to us in Luke 22:24-27.

3. Malcolm Muggeridge.

4. Hankey is quoted here from William Barclay, *The Gospel of John* in *The Daily Study Bible Series* (Philadelphia: The Westminster Press, 1975), p. 140.

11
Hope in the Answer to God's Call

I was walking through the cafeteria at the hospital the other day when I heard, "Steve!" I turned around to see a tall, husky, mustachioed young man with a grin on his face, walking toward me with his hand outstretched. I didn't know him from Adam.

He said, "You don't remember me, do you? I'm Derwin Alexander." I certainly remembered Derwin; I just did not recognize him from fifteen years ago. Derwin's dad used to pastor a church in a small town in which I worked as a youth minister at another church. I couldn't forget Derwin. Our youth groups were always getting together, and he had enough energy to cause himself to be remembered.

Derwin was in Waco scouting the job scene. He was a sales rep for an oil and gas outfit, and times were hard in this industry. He'd had his pay and benefits reduced and was afraid he could see the handwriting on the wall: It wouldn't be long before the whole company went down the tubes (pipelines?). He asked me if I knew of anything which might be a little more secure.

I made three calls for him. I called my brother (Southwestern Bell was not hiring), a friend of mine who is a vice president of development for a small, Christian, liberal-arts college (he had a job at $14,000 a year), and some salesmen friends for an office supply company. They were going to be in the office and invited Derwin to come by. There were no jobs in Waco, but there was an opening in Bryan/College Station. Derwin, with my buddies' help, arranged to talk to the sales manager for that territory.

I was telling Sally about this at the supper table. (Yep, that's what we call the PM meal in Texas. I am not without couth, however. I know some of you refer to this meal as "dinner.") She was glad to hear I had tried to help an old friend with whom she had grown up. Then she looked at me and said, "Do you realize how many people you have helped with jobs?"

It is true; I think I come by this concern honestly out of my own occupational tulmult. Many people are occupationally unhappy and frustrated. Perhaps you are one. I read and heard somewhere that only 10 percent of the populace are happy at their jobs. This is sad, seeing that we spend most of the waking lives at our employment. I have tried to help, in one way or another, everyone who has asked.

Part of my mental and spiritual turmoil in trying to find a satisfying job was the idealistic picture I had of the "right" occupation totally encompassing God's will for my life. For a long time, my idea of Christian vocation was that it was occupation. I assumed that if I could ever find that perfect job the struggle of trying to do God's will would be over. This was probably a carry-over from my pastorate days when, for me, this call was the ultimate. All of my abilities, energies, and interests were to be poured into this job or ignored. I have since decided occupation is important, but it is not primary. Christian voca-

tion is much deeper and broader than contentedly set-
tling into a job that makes us pleased as punch.

Work considerations do play a determining factor in
our lives, but our occupations do not contain the whole of
God's will. We cannot wait to get on with the business of
answering God's call until we find the perfect job. Christian vocation is much larger than mere occupation.

I hope, therefore, my contention to find a job with
which I am happy, and in which I am reasonably satisfied,
is not idolatry. A good job can never take God's place in
my life. I have been reminded of this as I have found hope
and strength only from my faith in Him in my futile
search for meaning. I have been forced to keep my occupational search in perspective by having it placed in the
larger framework of my call to Christian vocation.

*What does it mean, then, to answer God's call in our
lives? Or to put it another way: What is Christian vocation?*

*God's call is the call to show practical love to our family
and friends.*

I have often failed in showing patience, attention, and
time to my family because I was so frustrated over not
having the job which I had identified as the sum total of
God's will. I didn't know what this job was, of course. But
I knew it was out there somewhere! I have since decided
that giving some time, listening, and expressing love to
Sally and the kids is a big chunk of what it means for me
to answer God's call, regardless of where I am in the
search for the perfect job.

The importance of expressing practical love to my family was reaffirmed for me recently when Sally was talking
to her brother in Houston. Ike had been visiting with
them, trying to get in a little fun before school started.

Sally's brother was talking about Ike's visit with them, and he said to tell me, "That boy idolizes his daddy." Idolized me? I couldn't believe it! I nearly burst out crying while I was preparing a bowl of cereal when she told me that! What a privilege! What an honor! I realized when I heard this how important he is to me and how important it is for me to express love to him now. Being his daddy is one of my most important responsibilities.

Ike does not care whether I'm a writer, singer, artist, businessman, lawyer, or Indian chief, you see. He just knows I am his daddy. I, as one of his parents, am one of the two most important people to him on this earth. Sally and I are the people from whom he gets his self-worth and his ability to trust in God. We are the people from whom he first received love and from whom he learns what it is like to love others. We are the people from whom he learns important things in life like hanging tough, discipline, and hard work. This is very important.

I can no longer justify outbursts at my family by blaming it on being so tense over trying to do God's will. It is God's will that I love Sally, Ike, and Andrea now. I cannot afford to wait until I achieve my career goals before I begin to express love to them. I pray God will help me, through all of my concerns to do and be something, to hold in high priority my desire to express love to my family. And I pray He will help me to do it because it is a critical part of what it means for me to answer God's call.

Up with spousehood and parenthood, oh, ye weary and discouraged people! There is more opportunity to give and receive love within the family than anywhere else on this disheartened globe! There is more comfort in a hug from daughter or son and in a good talk with spouse than in all the business deals in the world! These are the relationships which have been a great balm for my soul, and in which I have found a partial answer to fulfilling my Christian vocation.

God's call is the call to express our talents, abilities, and interests for God's glory.

To me, this is another way to communicate the art of practical love. But how do you discover these ineffable qualities, you ask? I have sometimes discovered my interests and abilities by simply observing where I spend my time. For instance, I have invested a great number of hours in this book. I wrote before I had the slightest idea whether it would ever be published. I did not discover I had writing ability and then proceed to write a nice little book. I spent time writing and then discovered through the encouragement of others that I might be able to communicate something. I think that you, too, might find some of your gifts and interests through observing the use of your time and in answering questions like: What is that for which I am willing to persevere? What is that which will not leave me alone?

But I have also discovered my abilities and interests through more formal means, such as career and aptitude testing. I have, in the last five or six years, become quite conversant with career planning and aptitude and interest assessment. I have read a number of books and taken several tests on these subjects. I recently went to the Southwest Career Development Center in Arlington, Texas, to try to get some help. I am an intense person, and the pain I have felt over trying to figure out my occupation was so great I just had to go. I needed the help, and I am glad I went. They told me some things about myself that I might not have otherwise known.

I rated high in artistic interests, such as music, dramatics, art, and writing, but had never pursued any of these fields. The only interest to which I had given formal expression was a moderately high one in public speaking, through the pastorate. One of the tests I took indicated that I had moderately dissimilar interests to most pastors, and yet I had tried to function as one for six years! My jobs in the business world have not been places where I could directly use my gifts either.

None of this has been easy, and my working life has been hard. Nearly every day has been a teeth-grinding exercise in self-discipline with little associated joy. Sue Engelland, of the center, said it was a wonder I hadn't blown apart long before now! The truth is that I have been near mortally wounded by my occupational distress. There are still times when the discomfort roars over me like an eight-foot breaker on Padre Island.

The saving grace for me in this is the freedom I have begun to allow myself to use my abilities and interests now, regardless of whether my occupation requires them of me. For instance, I started this book when I was an account executive with Southwestern Bell. I finished it while serving as director of development at Hillcrest Hospital. I had to write it. It was in me, and I wrote in answer to the urge. My feelings resembled a daughter's expression to her dad when she was commenting on the significance of art: "The object of art is not to make salable pictures. It is to save yourself."[1] I wrote to save myself—to express the compulsion to tell my story. I have to use my gifts for God's glory or the depression pours in over me like the London fog.

I used to have ideas and squelched them into oblivion because I couldn't believe I could have a good idea. But

I have decided I can and do. The affirmation I feel in
Christ has encouraged me to seek to do His will through
the use of my gifts and interests, whether or not anyone
else gives me permission. I must try to do His will in this
way. I am compelled, yes, even called.

There is no use to wait until someone gives me or you
permission to get started in the stewardship of our gifts.
We can do it now. The Father affirms us; our abilities and
interests are as valid and effective for His purpose as
anyone else's. If we can use them on the job for God's
glory, so be it. If not, we can do it somewhere else. It is
either this or die.

Those of us who are doing "holy work," you see, are not
just the pastors and occupational evangelists or mission-
aries but those who are actively involved in giving our
best to God as an expression of our love for Him. "Whatever you do in word or deed, do all in the name of the Lord
Jesus, giving thanks through Him to God the Father"
(Col. 3:17). I know of no better way to make a permanent
investment in God's kingdom than in the stewardship of
our gifts and interests for His glory.

"What about the call of God to a specific place or kind
of service?" you ask. I do not believe Christian vocation
can be tied into a preconceived intricate, detail-by-detail,
celestial map with "God's Job for You" on it. I know—
"We are His workmanship, created in Christ Jesus for
good works" (Eph. 2:10)—but this reference is to the
works of Christian service and not to a specific occupation.

My own experience has led me to this belief about
Christian vocation. I felt I was called to preach when I
was eighteen and never prepared for anything else. The
idea that I would ever do anything different was totally

foreign to me. I majored in religion at Baylor University, went straight into the Master of Divinity program at Southwestern Baptist Theological Seminary, and followed that with a Doctor of Ministry degree. My commitment to be a preacher dominated my life, even in the midst of tragedy. I pastored for seven years and then quit.

The call of God to communicate the gospel through the use of my talents and interests still dominates my life. I feel it was a mistake, though, to equate this call with a specific job, whether it was the pastorate or anything else. For me, there has been a difference between my Christian vocation—to love people and to use my gifts for God's glory—and occupation. If I get to use my gifts and abilities on the job, then I consider it as an integral part of my calling. If not, then I consider the job as a way to provide for me and my family. What matters is answering the call of God in my life to love folk and to use my gifts for Him.

The calling of God to us is, therefore, the call to love people and to use all that we are for God's glory. Frederick Buechner beautifully stated these two aspects of the Christian life:

> The kind of work God usually calls you to is the kind of work (a) that you need most to do and (b) that the world most needs to have done. If you really get a kick out of your work, you've presumably met requirement (a), but if your work is writing TV deodorant commercials, the chances are you've missed requirement (b). On the other hand, if your work is being a doctor in a leper colony, you have probably met requirement (b), but if most of the time you're bored and depressed by it, the chances are you have not only bypassed (a) but probably aren't helping your patients much either.
>
> Neither the hair shirt nor the soft berth will do. The place God calls you to is the place where your deep gladness and the world's deep hunger meet.[2]

I have faith God is with me in every step of the pilgrimage of trying to grow to love people and to be a steward of my gifts and abilities for His glory. My way has not been a straight-line journey into peace and service. I have struggled for most of the trip. I would not have made it had not my loving Father illumined the way with the reflections of His grace. I have found strength for the pilgrimage in God's presence and hope for the future in believing He is somehow going to work all of this out for His glory and my highest good. I desire that you also find hope in His calling and a fellowship in His Presence that makes the trip worthwhile; it is, you know. He is with us all the way as we learn to love and to use our best for Him.

Notes

1. Anonymous, *Dear Dad* (Norwalk, Conn.: C. R. Gibson, 1927), pages are not numbered.

2. Frederick Buechner, *Wishful Thinking* (New York: Harper and Row, 1973), p. 95.